MYSTERY OR MAGIC

Biblical replies to the heterodox

© Copyright Rodney Schofield 2004

All rights reserved. No part of this publication may be reproduced, stored in a retrieval system, or transmitted in any form or by any means, electronic, mechanical, photocopying, recording or otherwise, without prior permission from the publishers.

First published 2004 by
Kachere Series
PO Box 1037
Zomba
Malawi
kachere@globemw.net

Distributed outside Africa by
African Books Collective
www.africanbookscollective.com

ISBN: 99908-16-60-3

Layout: Gladys Phiri
Graphic Design: Patrick Lichakala
Cover Design: Mercy Chilunga

Cover Illustration: Adoration of the Magi
(Church of Debra Sina Maryam, Gorgora, Ethiopia)

Quotations from the O.T. and N.T. are mainly from the Revised Standard Version, and those from the Apocrypha are from the Revised English Bible.

Printed by Lightning Source

MYSTERY OR MAGIC

Biblical replies to the heterodox

Rodney Schofield

Kachere Text no. 16

CONTENTS

Chapter 1: Facing the Issues
1. Introduction — 5
2. The Perennial Challenge — 10
3. Reformation England — 17
4. Apartheid South Africa — 22
5. Malawi Today — 24
6. Post-Modern Society — 31

Chapter 2: Faith and Falsehood in the Old Testament
1. Divination in Ancient Israel — 38
2. Methods of Divination — 41
3. Prophetic Inspiration — 44
4. Dreams — 48
5. Visions — 51
6. Malpractices — 54

Chapter 3: Life's Uncertainties in Hebrew Perspective
1. Sickness and Suffering — 57
2. The Role of Ritual — 63
3. The Shadow of Death — 70
4. Spiritual Powers at Work — 75

Chapter 4: Christian Affirmations
1. Deliverance from Evil — 83
2. The Promise of Abundance — 92
3. The Risen Lord — 98
4. Alive in Christ — 102
5. Heavenly Realities — 106

Chapter 5: Boundaries of Belief
1. The Riches of God's Glory — 113
2. The Spirit of Truth — 119
3. The Limits of Inculturation — 127

Chapter 1

Facing the Issues

Introduction

Before starting work as a missionary priest in Malawi (following a similar calling further south in Africa in the 1980s) I had imagined that witchcraft beliefs and practices would by now be marginalized, perhaps lingering on only in the more remote rural areas. Christianity after all was introduced into the country in the late nineteenth century, and is now well-established, with a high proportion of the population attending church fairly regularly. Primary schooling too is – at least in theory[1] – universally available, and a wider world of ideas has had time to make some impact. My initial assumptions were, however, quickly dispelled as I learnt of the fears that so many entertained of sorcery being used against them, and of the prevalence of protective magic. I was further surprised to learn from some of our theological students that even ordained ministers are known to carry charms on their persons (as in medieval Europe even priests are known to have carried *anethum graveolens* i.e. dill for the same purpose, exceeding the merely hygienic), and to hear that there are still many parts of the country where witchfinders are active and superstition is rife. In fact, had I read more widely I need not have been so unprepared. In the early 1970's it was observed by researchers "that the centre of interest is shifting from the traditional religious practices, such as offerings to the ancestral spirits, towards a type of pseudo-religion dominated by magic and belief in witchcraft"[2], illustrating the fact that popular forms of religion do not necessarily die out, but are prone to mutate. A letter to *The Tablet* in October 2002 by Fr. Piet Korse of Jinja, Uganda noted that "a deep-seated belief in witchcraft is at the root of much suffering in Africa".

However, it has further become evident that neither ordinands nor Christian ministers in the field see at all clearly the nature of their response. The situation is problematic, but the prevailing attitude seems to be one of slightly uneasy co-existence, rather than any form of challenge or confrontation, which seems to have characterised much missionary enterprise in the past.

---

[1] The latest (2002) recorded drop-out rate is 75%.
[2] Fr. J. Van Breugel reporting a conversation with J.M. Schoffeleers, in *Chewa Traditional Religion (Blantyre, 2001)*.

Where there has been, for example, a significant Calvinist element in the missionary stance this has been inevitable, as a doctrine of total depravity leaves little room for toleration let alone cultural adaptation. But the insensitivity can be overstated somewhat unfairly, since there are also sufficient examples of those who have stood alongside the indigenous people against the ruthlessness of traders and settlers, as well as many who have thought it necessary first to understand local customs before ever judging them[3]. In not a few areas western missionaries have made notable contributions to the study of both language and culture. But even the most renowned of all, the notably accommodating Jesuits in East Asia in the 16th and 17th centuries, were in the end discriminating: Matteo Ricci, for example, well known for his sympathetic appreciation of Confucian wisdom in China, would not tolerate what he thought to be superstitious practices[4]. Nor, in Africa and elsewhere, does it necessarily take years of patient research to observe fear and cruelty, not to mention human sacrifice and cannibalism, whatever the positive effects of customary belief may be.

There are political factors in Malawi as well: a swing towards pluralism and greater personal freedom, which has also helped to influence religious perspectives. With the advent of multi-party democracy in 1994, after thirty years of dictatorship, itself preceded by colonial rule, it might in fact be said that Malawi has its own version of post-modernism. It is significant that under the rule of Dr. Banda research into traditional practices was generally suppressed, as part of his policy of presenting a modernising state to the outside world. Hence tolerance is now seen as a virtue much to be prized. Yet it clearly has weaknesses of its own, such as a tendency towards the emasculating creed of relativism: "all have won, and all shall have prizes". It is certainly unfashionable in the more advanced post-modernism of the west to be dogmatic, and there the prime Christian virtue is considered to be "affirmation" of the other person. In fact, it is regarded as religious imperialism - an affront to his or her human rights, with legislation actually in the wings - to challenge the values that someone else holds or practises.

So too one senses that in Africa the very word "missionary" can carry unwelcome overtones - and for understandable reasons: commerce, colonialisation (which is effectively what David Livingstone's term

---

[3] Among those worthy of mention in Malawi are Dr. Robert Laws (Presbyterian), William Johnson (Anglican) and Fr. Claude Boucher (Catholic).

[4] For example, Ricci forbade converts to make petitions to the dead, condemning the belief that they received any benefit through food offerings or the burning of paper money.

"civilisation" came to mean) and Christianity did all too often go hand in hand, and, despite some undoubted benefits to the African, there were many wrongs inflicted[5]. In particular, there is a prevailing assumption that traditional religion was attacked, and traditional culture undermined, before ever the attempt was made to evaluate them properly. Hence, in the face of continually encroaching westernisation and with widening gaps between rich and poor in the world (and within Malawi itself), whatever now remains of the "African worldview" is felt to be a heritage not to be eroded lightly. The old ways condemned by the missionaries are regarded in some quarters (for example, in theses on moral theology prepared during 2000 and subsequent years by several Catholic seminarians from the Phalombe district) as the key to restoring family and community life[6]. Other Christian students are prepared to challenge the insistence upon monogamy, or to call for a re-evaluation of sexual ethics, seeing them as imposed by foreigners while being alien to their own culture. The slogan "Africa for the Africans" is a popular one, applied more widely than simply within the context of land redistribution.

There is some confusion here between what is of Biblical origin and what is of more recent, possibly secular, derivation. The reaction against western lifestyles does not usually distinguish too carefully between, for example, Christian values and European or American culture (admittedly not always a distinction appreciated by missionaries themselves). The antipathy means too that rigorous theological critique may be impaired. "The reluctance to accept the changes of time and their unavoidable consequences has many variants. Criticism against modernisation is one of them, another is the almost canonising approach of contemporary African theologians towards African Traditional Religions. Any romanticism towards the African past can be understood from a human point of view, but it is unacceptable when we look at the problems that have to be addressed with regard to the development of

---

[5] Contemporary writers were not unmindful of the ills. There is a splendid example in A.Trollope's *Framley Parsonage* of 1860, the year in which Charles MacKenzie and others were responding to Livingstone's call for a mission to Central Africa: at Bishop Proudie's suggestion that Christianity, along with "guidance, encouragement, instruction", was useful for the natives, the journalist Mr. Supplehouse, "the business of whose life it had been to suggest difficulties", pointed out that in America "we exterminated the people instead of civilizing them."

[6] Traditional birth control among the Lomwe people is for the woman to wear a belt of beads and herbs. A local Indian lady doctor told me she has not yet observed its efficacy among her pregnant patients: "perhaps next time", they say.

African societies towards large-scale communities."[7] Indeed there is an over-eagerness to claim that African religion is a precursor of Christian faith, and in many respects compatible with it, so that the task of theology is to recast its thinking in an African mould. "Christ was in Africa before Christianity" is the new watchword, taken by some to mean that the intellectual baggage of apostolic (or patristic, or scholastic, or reformed, ...) teaching is superfluous. Certainly some of the African Initiated Churches manage to achieve a popular blend of ancestral beliefs and sacrifices with merely a hint of Christian overtones, although others again are fairly ruthless in exorcising the past.

In present-day Malawi there is no dearth of studies of traditional culture and its interaction with the Christian churches, for which every credit is due. Yet while in the past assumptions and generalisations about African society were all too common, it now seems that this weakness applies in reverse. The "Biblical point of view" is too readily taken for granted, when in reality it is just as complex as the indigenous phenomena with which it is being compared. Ideas about this life and the next (if any), about spiritual powers, about combating evil, about divination and contact with the divine, went through much change and development, not least because of the contacts between Israel and her neighbours. It is not true that there is always a well-defined, and perhaps inflexible, position in the Bible on all of these issues. The picture is many-layered, and it should be noted that what emerged as the Christian stance, so far as it can be identified, had already undergone critical thinking and interaction with other religious beliefs and philosophies both before and after the time of Christ, with similar exposure in the centuries of theological debate to follow.

The fundamental claim of Christians is expressed best of all in the words of St. Paul: "In all these things we are more than conquerors through him who loved us. For I am sure that neither death, nor life, nor angels, nor principalities, nor things present, nor things to come, nor powers, nor height, nor depth, nor anything else in all creation, will be able to separate us from the love of God in Christ Jesus our Lord" (Rom 8.37-39). The powers and forces - elemental spirits of the universe (Col 2.8) - so often feared are in fact unable to harm us: they have already been disarmed by Christ on the Cross (Col 2.15). The basic conviction, to which Paul gave eloquent and varied expression, is that, no matter what overarching cosmology may be preferred (Jewish or Greek, primitive or scientific ...) the hostile world around us or within us has met its match in Christ.

---

[7] Martin Ott: *Inculturation in the African city (The Lamp 23 - Balaka, Malawi, 2000)*

How was this position reached? I hope to explore this question by surveying the relevant material in both Old and New Testaments, together with rather briefer excursions into the Apocrypha - recognising that this cannot be neglected in seeking to understand the development of Biblical ideas. But what is the relevant material? Before commencing this Biblical survey in the next and succeeding chapters, I offer a rapid historical sketch of the varied interactions between church and society in such matters as witchcraft and divination, with several more detailed illustrations including the current fascination with all things occult in the west. These will be seen to raise deeper questions about underlying causes and the kind of climate in which heterodox ideas seem to flourish.

It certainly needs to be registered that in the area of "alternative religion", as with other factors impinging upon the Church's mission, each new generation poses fresh issues, challenges and difficulties. It is evident that in matters of superstition a time-chart is for ever recording peaks and troughs. Sorcery and magic may in a particular age seem to dwindle to nothing, only to be found flourishing with new vigour a century or two later, as might be true too of some infectious disease. Indeed, the analogy has a certain aptness in so far as diseases can be fought almost to the point of extinction by every medical expedient, only to mutate into new and stubbornly resistant strains (for example, malaria or sleeping sickness). Thus, where once Evans-Pritchard, one of the outstanding anthropologists of the early 20th century, could posit a "pre-logical" or "mystical" mentality that although relatively self-consistent would die out as modernity overtook the Azande people, whom he had studied in Central Africa, the mystical and magical are now seen more often as parasitic upon conventional orthodoxies, or at least as a reaction to contemporary events and circumstances. There is a plausible thesis that unrest and uncertainty, as well as distrust and envy, are significant factors behind these phenomena. "Witches are modernity's prototypical malcontents", embodying "all the contradictions of the experience of modernity itself"[8]. Surely, then, we must note that these "contradictions" call as much for Christian response as the errors into which people may fall. Hence attention will be given in the following chapters, not only to heterodox deviations from beliefs and practices regarded as normative, but also to the underlying issues of sin and evil, suffering and death, and the Biblical reactions and remedies which offer more effective answers to them. It may perhaps appear that some aspects of Biblical truth, insufficiently appreciated in Africa, are also less familiar than they should be in western countries, with

---

[8] Comaroff and Comaroff: *Modernity and its Malcontents (Chicago, 1993)*

the potential to address a like age of doubt and insecurity.

I am under no illusions, however, that this is an unfashionable position to take: Biblical fundamentalists may not wish to sift the evidence, while those of more liberal persuasion would dismiss the exercise as outdated and irrelevant! As Cardinal Ersilio Tonini has recently commented: "Contemporary society is locked in a perverse game. Since it has lost all hope, there is only cynicism, the Nietzschean quest for omnipotence, the desire for infinite development. Christianity, by contrast, is still trying to say words which everyone else has forgotten – 'yes' and 'no', 'good' and 'bad'. The church was born as a counterculture, and today it finds itself so once more."

The Perennial Challenge

When the people of Israel entered the promised land (in so far as the conversion to Yahwism was effected by tribal immigration), it was not empty: Canaanite religion was already in place, and it continued to flourish, as did popular superstition, alongside the worship of Yahweh for many centuries. When the early church emerged from Judaism, it faced the task of clarifying its essential beliefs and characteristics: in the process it aroused much hostility from Jewish quarters, which put in jeopardy the limited protection given by the state while Christianity was still regarded as a Jewish sect. In passing, one may note that for their part the Jews commonly accused Jesus of being himself a magician, which may explain why St. Matthew in his Gospel dropped the Marcan references (Mk 7.33;8.23) to Jesus' use of spittle, given its magical associations. Again, when St. Paul promoted the Gospel within the Graeco-Roman world, the need became apparent to appraise a whole variety of philosophies and life-styles, not properly encountered in Palestine itself. Yet his watchword remained, "Do not be conformed to this world, but be transformed by the renewal of your mind" (Rom 12.2). And in every subsequent expansion of the church, these basic issues remained: what is the *esse* of the Christian faith, how is it best expressed in a particular society, and what elements of an existing culture remain compatible with it? There is the further (and vital) pastoral issue: in so far as the Gospel imposes its own requirements, how gently or how stridently are they to be introduced? Do allowances need to be made for human weakness in accepting change, suggesting a policy of "accommodation" to accompany any necessary confrontation? Or must accommodation only be seen as compromise, given that the Bible in both its testaments is generally uncompromising towards occult practices, magic and witchcraft (as detailed below), and that from apostolic times the Church has campaigned[9] fairly steadily against recourse to the supernatural, apart from its own principled use of prayer and sacrament?

In the early centuries augury and sortilege were favourite targets, despite the casting of lots in the appointment of Judas Iscariot's successor (Acts 1.26). With the circulation of Biblical codices it is a little surprising to note the development of *sortes Biblicae*, a seeking of divine guidance by opening a codex and reading a verse at random. Although St. Augustine of Hippo was prompted to mend his own life as a result of doing this, he later wrote against the practice: it was at least better than resorting to other forms of divination, he thought, but it tended to turn the mind away from higher things to "the vanities of the present life". Various synods subsequently condemned it, and indeed excommunicated any involved in it. Augustine's view of occult beliefs in general was that conversion and education were the preferred steps forward. The broad concurrence of his contemporaries can be gauged from the widespread shock that followed the first known execution (in 385 AD) of a Christian, Priscillian of Avila, on account of his heretical "witchcraft". His death, however, was not the outcome of a heresy hunt so much as an opportunity seized by an aspiring Roman general Magnus Maximus to stake his own orthodox (Nicene) credentials; Priscillian's accusers, two Spanish bishops, were eventually deprived of their sees.

Christian art of this period also has one or two surprises, in that scenes from pagan mythology can often be found (for example, on the mosaic floors of Roman villas, or decoratively carved on artefacts) juxtaposed with Christian themes and symbols. A century or two later Pope Gregory the Great is well-known for his apparent endorsement of "inculturation"; he responded to Augustine (of Canterbury)'s anxieties about pagan practices in Britain by urging him to "baptise" them into the church, wherever possible. With some Druidical practices this was of course out of the question, and the Roman administration itself had earlier put a stop to human sacrifices. But there is the point often overlooked: even where customs could be Christianised this might only be a temporary expedient to allow the leaden attitudes of British people time to adapt! "It is doubtless impossible," wrote Gregory, "to cut out

---

[9] At its very inception the Church's stance against the official practices of the Roman world attracted counter-charges of impiety and atheism. Suetonius, for example, gives favourable mention to Nero's attack on the Christians of Rome in the 60s, considering them guilty, among other things, of "black magic" – an accusation often repeated in the later 2nd century, and one not unknown in subsequent missionary encounters.

everything at once from their stubborn minds." So the Venerable Bede (who died in 735 AD) could fittingly regard his instruction as a realistic accommodation to the pace of possible change. In fact the Latin church was generally of the opinion that even when false gods and pagan practices had been publicly overthrown, they lingered tenaciously in the hearts of all too many Christians. "The question is sometimes put why the Anglo-Saxons were converted to Christianity so quickly. The truth is that they were not converted at all quickly. In spite of there being good political and cultural reasons for the conversion of kings to Christianity, in spite of able and saintly missionaries, it took nearly ninety years to convert just the kings and the greater part of their aristocracy, not to speak of the countryside which was a question of centuries. In the course of that ninety years hardly a court was converted which did not suffer at least one subsequent relapse into paganism before being reconverted. The old religious instincts died hard."[10]

Bede's *Ecclesiastical History of the English People* is the principal source for much of this period. As one who spent almost his entire life in the monasteries of Wearmouth and Jarrow, he is particularly informative about preaching endeavours in the north and records a number of stories about St. Cuthbert and others as they engaged with popular beliefs and superstitions. On one occasion, he relates, "mock fire" was sent down by the devil to interfere with Cuthbert's work: "Sheets of flame, fanned by the wind, seemed to sweep through the whole village, and the noise of their crackling rent the air. Cuthbert managed, with outstretched arms, to restrain a few of the villagers, but the rest, almost the whole crowd, leaped up and vied with each other in throwing water on the flames. But real water has no effect on phantom fire, and the blaze raged on, until through Cuthbert's prayers the father of lies fled, taking his false fire with him into the empty air."

In 786 AD the legates sent to England from papal Rome commented on the survival of pagan magic, and Alcuin, in a letter to the Archbishop of York, subsequently pointed out that some people still carried magic amulets and were "taking to the hills where they worship, not with prayer, but in drunkenness". Both St. Wilfred and St. Cuthbert seem to have met much hostility from pagan priests and their followers: "they have robbed us of the old religion and nobody knows how to cope with all these changes". However, no missionary to the Anglo-Saxons is known to have been martyred, and this may be a testimony to the wisdom of Gregory's accommodating policy. It may reflect also the fact that in some measure the

---

[10] Henry Mayr-Harting: *The Coming of Christianity to Anglo-Saxon England* (London, 1972)

missionaries were impressive as holy men, able in peasant eyes to work their own form of "magic" – the need for which Gregory himself was well aware when he send wonder-working relics[11], such as filings from St. Peter's chains, to barbarian princes. "Pagans expected gifts from the gods in exchange for the gifts which men offered to them ... The ambassadors of Christianity could offer no less. They, too, had to produce victory in battle, good crops, many children, deliverance from disease and death: or at least to produce the necessary impression."[12] In this vein of thinking the 8th century bishop Daniel of Winchester wrote to St. Boniface, a fellow archbishop in heathen lands beyond the river Rhine (who was in fact martyred, in 755 AD), "We Christians possess lands rich in oil and wine and abounding in other resources, but the gods have left to the pagans lands stiff with cold".

Somewhat later in Europe, Charlemagne, in line with earlier imperial powers, was less content with persuasion, or even counter-propaganda; he condemned occult beliefs as evil, and passed severe laws against them, including the death penalty. Others saw these things merely as a contemptible relic of paganism; indeed, among the Germanic peoples, who spread throughout Europe after the decline of the Roman Empire, fear of witchcraft was common. Around 900 AD *Canon Episcopi* taught that only infidels believed in witches, but penalties were comparatively lenient, Pope Nicholas 1 having prohibited the use of any torture. In the popular mind it began to be thought that heretics were in league with the devil, leading them to abortion, infanticide and cannibalism. Regino of Prum noted that *innumera multitudo* believed the wild assertions, and thus, he said, "departed from the true faith". Hence it was "the duty of priests earnestly to instruct the people that these things are absolutely untrue and that such imaginings are planted in the minds of unbelieving folk, not by a divine spirit, but by the spirit of evil".

However, contact with the Arab world introduced new studies in the 12th century such as alchemy and astrology. The outstanding scholar Roger Bacon, who worked in the newly founded universities of Oxford and Paris, was fascinated by the teachings of astrology, and is regarded by some as a scientist born out of time. He certainly proposed the experimental method as a more reliable means of advancing knowledge than mere metaphysical speculation. Although astrology is now regarded as a pseudo-science, this is only with the benefit of hindsight, resulting from what Thomas Kuhn memorably termed "a paradigm shift": it does have a certain intellectual appeal, until one accepts that its predictive value cannot be upheld

---

[11] See *Excursus* later in this section.
[12] David L. Edwards: *Christian England (London, 1981)*

empirically. The impact of these new interests led to the notion of magic as a mere "peasant superstition" being undermined, even allowing the idea that there might be a beneficial aspect of witchcraft itself, for example, in curing sickness. Bacon argued for a rational examination of its truth.

In the 13th century theologians such as Bacon's protagonist St. Thomas Aquinas (*Summa I.51*) began to address these concerns once again, and papal letters (e.g. Gregory IX's *Vox in Rama* of 1233) were issued warning of the dangers of the occult. Canon lawyers subsequently entered the fray with manuals on how to extract confessions, but it was agitation against heretics that finally caused a change in church policy. There were witch trials in the south of France directed against the Cathari, or Albigensian heretics, with some burned to death and others imprisoned for life. Allegations of Satanism, including practice of the Black Mass, were made against the Knights Templar in the 14th century, while from this period onwards inquisition records begin to mention the Witches' Sabbath, a midnight assembly held in fealty to the devil. An important decision seems to have been made in the theological faculty at Paris in 1395 that witchcraft was an offence against Christian faith, namely, idolatry or devil worship. The notion quickly then took hold that all activities of witches were an inversion of normal Christian behaviour. It should be noted though that this was also the time when hospitals for the insane were being founded in Spain, so that not all bizarre behaviour was accounted intrinsically malevolent. Meanwhile in England, the duchess of Gloucester was given life imprisonment for making a wax image of king Henry VI and then melting it down; her accomplices were executed in the most painful ways imaginable. In a key development of 1484 two Dominican friars, Heinrich Kraemer and Johann Sprenger, persuaded Innocent VIII to publish a bull against witchcraft in Germany; two years later they themselves issued *Malleus Maleficarum,* an encyclopaedia of demonology that became the standard reference work for the next three centuries. It attempted to show in a systematic way how the power of witches derived from their links (often described as sexual) with the devil: "the godless by their deeds and words have asked Hades for his company" (Wis 1.16) was interpreted as meaning a close association with the devil. After the Reformation, Protestant leaders zealously pursued their own campaigns, Martin Luther in particular demanding the extermination of witches, more on doctrinal than on social grounds; and, although down the centuries there were always sceptics urging restraint (not least the Jesuit Friedrich von Spee who in 1631 published *Cautio Criminalis*), the mania did not really abate until medieval cosmology was replaced by the less theocratic frame of reference of the modern world.

Excursus: anomalous Church practices?

To the modern mind looking back over this period, certain anomalies appear. Some practices acceptable to the medieval Church, such as the devotion to saintly relics, may strike us today (as they indeed struck Luther) as bordering upon the magical; and we may begin to wonder if the difference between a relic and a charm (or between white magic and black magic) might not lie mostly in the political realm i.e. in the degree of control that the Church was able to exercise.

Nevertheless, it is perhaps worth noting a few of the Biblical and historical landmarks which have led at least some Christians to treasure these tangible associations with sanctity. There is in the Old Testament a stern reminder of the powerful *mana* of sacred objects: in Numbers 4.15ff, the sons of Kohath are warned that "they must not touch the holy things, lest they die", and even looking upon them is too dangerous (v20). In 2 Samuel 6.6-11 Uzziah is punished for touching the ark of God; whereas by contrast Obed-edom the Gittite is then blessed for keeping it safe for the following three months. 2 Kings 13.21 relates the wonder-working efficacy of Elisha's bones (below, 3.3), perhaps anticipating two remarkable stories in the New Testament. First, in the Gospels (Mt 9.20-22; Mk 5.25-34; Lk 8.43-48) a woman with a haemorrhage touches Jesus' garments, and through her faith, later commended by Jesus, is made well; "power" had "gone forth" from him. Secondly, Luke – ever eager to show parallels between the life of the early Church and that of Jesus himself – records this in Acts 19.11-12: "And God did extraordinary miracles by the hands of Paul, so that handkerchiefs and aprons were carried away from his body to the sick, and diseases left them and the evil spirits came out of them."

The later age of martyrs saw the beginning of saintly veneration; at first a localised devotion, but one which, especially after the Decian persecution in the mid 3rd century, grew to such proportions that official Church control was needed. Typical is this comment made after Polycarp's martyrdom (probably 156 AD): his bones were considered "more valuable than precious stones and more excellent than gold". When the peace of Constantine ushered in the possibility of Christian pilgrimage in the 4th century, it was his mother Helena who claimed (around 326 AD) to have found relics of the true cross in Jerusalem. Holy artifacts and saintly bones were felt by many to have retained numinous power through their intimate association with holy persons; an "incarnational" belief not discouraged by leading bishops such as Ambrose (who himself was led through a dream to find forgotten bones) and Augustine. One much treasured relic in the west was the remains of St. Martin's cloak or cape, after he had given the rest to a beggar; on Martin's death in 397 AD a "chapel" was built where the Frankish kings kept this "capella". Elsewhere it became common, and indeed necessary, for an altar to house a relic within it (cf Rev 6.9), and for collections of relics to be made – each one, perhaps, suggestive of different spiritual (and, increasingly, material) benefits; but at this very point in danger of usurping the sacramental blessings promised by Christ to his Church.

To his credit, Augustine was alive to the fraudulent claims made of some "saintly" remains, and in 401 a North African council insisted on more rigorous authentication. During this same period, there is one radical protest that has survived, that of Vigilantius, a priest of Acquitaine: "We almost see the rites of the pagans introduced into the churches under the guise of religion ... everywhere people kiss and adore some bit of dust in a little pot, wrapped in a precious fabric." When Jerome received this document in Bethlehem, he gave it a scathing reply: one must not restrict God's sovereign power! Hence it is not surprising to learn that by the 8th century the trade in relics had grown quite out of hand, with bodies of earlier saints and martyrs being broken up for commerce. It has been observed, "If we were able to draw up statistics of imports into England in the 10th century, relics would certainly come high on the list". Indeed, by this time papal authority itself owed less to scriptural and historical claims than to the fact that the very body of St. Peter rested in Rome; while guide books to Rome and elsewhere became little other than catalogues of the relics to be found. One of the most remarkable events was at Chartres in 1194, when the Romanesque cathedral burnt down, leaving the "veil" of the Blessed Virgin Mary unscathed; a seeming miracle which inspired a rapid rebuilding programme, and, of course, an even greater influx of pilgrims. From the 14th century onwards the guide books began to list the indulgences attached to veneration of particular relics: "Then people long to go on pilgrimages / And palmers long to see the stranger strands / Of far-off saints, hallowed in sundry lands."[13]

It is no coincidence that the day chosen by Luther in 1517 to promulgate his ninety-five theses, criticising contemporary Catholic distortions of the faith, was 31st October, the eve of All Saints' Day: for on the following day, the Elector Frederick was as usual to expose his magnificent collection of relics in the castle church of Wittenberg, with indulgences promised to those faithful

---

[13] G.Chaucer: *The Canterbury Tales*

Christians who might piously attend. His protest was overdue, opening up a more searching scrutiny of the Church's teaching and practice. All too easily failings could be blamed upon heretics and witches, but what if the fault –line ran through the Church itself? Calvin was scathing in his criticisms of official practice, which had (in one example) been "imposing on the rude and ignorant, by displaying a piece of common wood as the wood of the Cross, they have declared it every way worthy of adoration. This doctrine is altogether devilish." In the ensuing Catholic Reformation, the Council of Trent summed up its position in judicious words focusing on *human* relics: "The holy bodies of the holy martyrs and others living with Christ, whose bodies were living members of Christ and temples of the Holy Spirit, and will be by him raised to eternal life and glorified, are to be venerated by the faithful, since by them God [*explicitly the author of the miracles in Acts 19.11*] bestows many benefits upon men." There is no indication here that those lacking faith will receive such benefits (cf Mk 5.25ff). Pius V at that time reduced the number of saints' celebrations considerably, although of course they increased again later. Another landmark later on was the work of the 18th century Ludovico Muratori, who in *Della regolata devozione dei cristiani* advocated a form of scriptural religiosity that eschewed any reliance upon superstitious or quasi-magical attachments. More recently (1969), the Calendar was under Paul VI again simplified, expunging a number of "unhistorical" saints. Greater emphasis is now placed upon the inspirational and exemplary lives of the saints ("the wonderful works of Christ in his servants", as Vatican II expressed it) than upon their miraculous assistance. It may be noted too that the dispersal of relics into small pieces, and the formation of relic collections, has of late been strongly condemned by the Vatican Congregation for Divine Worship.

But in Reformation days can it be said that the much stricter Protestant line, dismissing altogether the miracles and even the memories of holy men and women, brought nothing but gain?

Reformation England

There was in 16th and early 17th century England a remarkable upsurge in witchcraft accusations. The classic study is that of Keith Thomas: *Religion and the Decline of Magic (Harmondsworth, 1971)*. He attributes it to two principal, but related factors: one is the birth of the Church of England, and the other is the rise of Protestant individualism. He argues that when misfortune struck and uncanny things happened in earlier times, the Catholic

Church had its own armoury of protection: relics, pilgrimages, the prayers of the saints, allied with the power of exorcism. Holding no brief to argue for their efficacy, and certainly without attempting to appraise their theological validity, he observes that in their absence the ordinary Christian was left feeling vulnerable. It was a time when the social, as well as the religious world, was being challenged and changed. Growing prosperity for some left others behind: hence there were those who felt guilty about the disparities of wealth, so that it was typically the poor neighbour turned away at the door whose subsequent curse was most feared and against whose vulnerability witchcraft accusations were often successful - for who, after all, of any influence would defend them? In time the poor laws came to offer some collective relief by the parish, eventually supplanted by the modern welfare state, thus quietening the consciences of the more affluent.

The rise of science, promoted by men such as Francis Bacon and later John Wilkins (who helped to form the Royal Society in 1660), in an age of growing "enlightenment" for its part also helped in due course to undermine the credibility of occult powers and the *modus operandi* through which it might be supposed they were able to control the affairs of men and women. An early counterblast was that of Reginald Scot, who in 1584 wrote his *Discovery of Witchcraft,* which dismissed the exploits of so-called witches as so much nonsense. But in 1604 a fierce anti-witchcraft statute was passed by Parliament, and one may note the performance at the royal court two years later of Shakespeare's anti-witchcraft play *Macbeth.* As James VI of Scotland, James I had been fascinated by the subject, and had written a treatise on *Demonology* - although in England his interest waned when he found that some of the better educated people regarded the subject with amusement. Nevertheless, for the next half-century at least, "enlightened" views such as Scot's had little noticeable effect, with hundreds of witches (mainly women) suffering imprisonment or death, especially during the virulent campaign of Matthew Hopkins in the 1640s. Eventually the educated classes grew more cautious, and ceased pursuing legal charges against those accused of involvement in the so-called "black arts". The critical approaches of science, initially thought by many to be merely a new form of magic, gained in respectability and came to influence public consciousness, so that the execution of Alice Molland at Exeter in 1685 marked the effective end of the witch-hunting epoch, officially declared over in 1736 when witchcraft was removed as a crime from the statute-books. However, one should observe that even in his later years the great Isaac Newton continued secretly dabbling in alchemy, just as sophisticated scientists today can combine curiously unconventional ideas with their professional studies.

Prior to the Restoration period, Thomas observes that there was no compelling reason for distinguishing between remedies that were officially sanctioned and the practices of cunning men and women, diviners, or supposed witches. Contemporary medicine was too often a painful, but unfruitful, faith in purges and blood-lettings, while it was by no means obvious that a Protestant minister had any more influence with the unseen forces than his Catholic counterpart: indeed some complained that of old "churchmen had more cunning and could teach people many a trick that our ministers nowadays know not." Their true rival was the village wizard, who at least performed with panache in dispensing his charms and spells, a not-unimportant psychological factor. What has been termed "the therapeutic power of the imagination" is undoubtedly a force to be reckoned with, and in less-advanced societies (Thomas mentions the emerging African countries of today), as also in more sophisticated western countries, results count! In a world that has not yet infallibly conquered pain, hardship, suffering and death, any ally is worth having in the fight. So Thomas argues from his historical studies that, whether from a religious, or a medical, or a scientific point of view, any who claim to monopolise salvation will never lack for competition. And the competition may not always be negligible: the keeper of Canterbury gaol in 1570 gave privileges to an inmate on the grounds that "the witch did more good by her physic than Mr. Pundall and Mr. Wood, being preachers of God's word".

In a sermon preached in 1552, Bernard Gilpin commented on the extent to which magic had survived the religious changes of the early Tudor period in England. "What gross superstition and blindness remaineth still among the people only through lack of faithful preachers. Infidelity, idolatry, sorcery, charming, witchcrafts, conjuring, trusting in figures, with other such trumpery … lurk in corners and began of late to come abroad, only for lack of preaching." Thomas notes wryly, "Faithful preachers were indeed the deadly enemies of such practices, but Gilpin was wrong to imply that the clergy could ever hope to triumph by mere exhortation." We hear later, for example, of a 17th century astrologer who confessed, "The truth is, after the ministers had preached against me and my art, I had twice so much custom as before, for they could not have done me better service; for many which before had not heard of me made much inquiring after me, hearing what great cures I had done." Nor was it only in rural areas that magical services were in demand. 17th century London was "not exempt from witchcraft accusations, and the city seems to have harboured every kind of popular magician", even though it might be considered more abreast of modern ideas and readier to test out extravagant claims. The sects with their prophecies and healing miracles flourished there; however, neighbourly charges and countercharges within the city were gradually on the wane, since in a population measured in hundreds of thousands anonymity was a growing reality.

Perhaps the most remarkable of all the magical survivals was "the King's touch". The mystique surrounding this went back to the time of Edward the Confessor, who instituted the practice in England. Many believed that "the King's evil" or scrofula (tubercular swelling of the lymph glands, probably caused by infected milk) could be healed by the monarch himself. Patients in earlier days had been advised to seek the king's aid only as a last resort, and after the Reformation some Protestant divines were intent to downplay the very idea of miracles happening. But the demand continued, with Reginald Scot commenting of Elizabeth I: "Her Majesty only useth godly and divine prayer, with some alms, and referreth the cure to God and the physician". Yet, despite the ironical comment of John Donne that ordinary cunning men or women who used the healing touch were prosecuted for sorcery, the King's touch reached its zenith under Charles II, who is believed to have laid his hand on over 90,000 people during his reign. The peak year was 1683, after which growing scepticism allied to a decline in the belief of the divine right of kings saw Queen Anne the last monarch to be sought for her touch. In France, the practice lived on for another century.

The suggestion has been made that, although religion and magic both addressed the questions of daily misfortune and suffering, and so were rivals for people's attention, in fact religious belief offered what popular magic and superstition could never aspire to; namely a coherent account of human life, experienced both this side of death and beyond it. Divine providence was the all-embracing doctrine in early modern England which could inform the understanding of every event, from an "accident" in the home to the defeat of the Spanish Armada. "Whereas the faith of the Christian", notes Thomas, "was a guiding principle, relevant to every aspect of life, magic was simply a means of overcoming various specific difficulties." Occult explanations never cohered into a systematic body of doctrine, despite certain 16th and 17th century attempts at achieving this, sometimes influenced by neo-Platonic ideas about the relationship between matter and spirit. Theology, by contrast, could be described as queen of the sciences, in so far as it proposed guiding principles within a comprehensive account of man's place in the universe. It might, however, sometimes suit the individual believer to give credence to an alternative explanation of his misfortune: "according to the Kentish gentleman, Henry Oxinden, it was precisely this refusal to endure the correction of God which led men [*including the clergy*] to blame their adversities upon some neighbour's witchcraft". Astrology too provided an easy way out of accepting personal responsibility before God, a point noted by Shakespeare in *King Lear*: "an admirable evasion of whoremaster man, to lay his goatish disposition to the charge of a star". But at least it agreed with the Christian faith in this: that life's set-backs and problems are not dealt out entirely capriciously, nor is the cosmos simply a chapter of accidents.

Excursus: witch-hunting in New England

From May to October of 1692 Salem in New England was in the grip of a witch-hunt. It began when a few young girls, stimulated by voodoo tales told by a West Indian slave, Tituba, made claims that they were possessed by the devil and subsequently accused three Salem women of witchcraft. Certainly the girls exhibited symptoms of convulsions and hallucinations, but it has been noted that these rather strikingly matched descriptions of supernatural phenomena to be found in the best-selling book *An Essay for the Recording of Illustrious Providences* published eight years earlier in Boston by the Congregational minister Increase Mather – a copy of which is known to have existed in the house where the trouble began. In the investigations that followed the accused falsely incriminated others until, in a climate of mass hysteria across Massachusetts, about 150 people found themselves in prison awaiting trial. The evidence adduced against them included claims that that they had been seen flying on broomsticks; that they had instructed bees to deposit nails in the stomachs of the children; that they had metamorphosed themselves into spectres. To their credit the clergy, including Mathers, who had demanded the investigations, pressured the court to reject these reports of spectres, on the grounds that a witch could assume the form of an innocent person. Although by now 19 people had been hanged, and one man slowly pressed to death under heavy stones when he refused to plead guilty to charges, public opinion began to change, and Governor William Phipps dissolved the court in October. The convictions were later annulled, and indemnities granted to the families of those who had been executed. However, only one of the three judges, Samuel Sewall (in the course of time to become a commissioner of SPG, my own missionary society), publicly admitted his error. It may be observed retrospectively that ministers like Increase Mathers lost considerable credibility for their outdated views of the supernatural.

It has been estimated that in the three hundred years from 1450 to 1750 some 60,000 people were executed in Europe or America for suspected witchcraft, of whom perhaps one quarter were men.

Apartheid South Africa

On a different continent and in a different century the ethnographer Isak Niehaus has written a fascinating book *Witchcraft, Power and Politics (Claremont, 2001)* which charts the history of witchcraft accusations in Northern Transvaal during the 1980s, at the height of the apartheid years. A crucial turning point for these rural communities seems to have been some 20 years earlier when resettlement plans were implemented, uprooting many people and imposing new forms of social life ("villagisation") upon them. "Whilst people's neighbours had always been their kin, their new neighbours were often complete strangers." Attributions of witchcraft escalated when strangers failed to meet the social obligations of neighbourliness. Nor was the situation helped by the Bantu Authorities Act, which weakened the chiefs' powers to resolve friction more or less peacefully, and by default eventually encouraged the ANC Comrades to intervene more violently.

Niehaus sees such attributions as a form of protest and resistance for the weak; as it were, a popular mode of political action. Witch-hunting is described as "a creative attempt to eliminate evil", but is at the same time an indirect warning to the rich and powerful to redistribute their wealth. "Villagers situationally invoke witchcraft beliefs as they encounter perplexing events, experience prolonged conflict in marriage, or suffer unspeakable misfortune... [Witchcraft] has less to do with civilisation [*i.e. culture*] and African identity than with their experiences of misery, marginalisation, illness, poverty and insecurity." The villagers under scrutiny were not prepared to account for their setbacks, deprivations or deaths simply in terms of impersonal processes such as unfavourable weather, outbreaks of contagious disease, or mechanical accident; nor would they regard the idea of "mere coincidences" as plausible. They also "clearly distinguished between social tensions in general and the types of tensions that they associated with witchcraft. In Green Valley individuals were regularly accused of being rapists, adulterers, thieves, sell-outs, arrogant or unbearable persons. Witchcraft does not refer to these visible actions, but denotes mystical deeds, motivated by envy, malice and resentment." Indeed, it was often the case that outwardly witches might appear to be "sociable, friendly, kind and hospitable", but at night, while others slept, they assumed the shape of a familiar, or else became invisible, to perpetrate their evil deeds.

And perhaps this instinct to look for human causes of suffering is at root a sound one. A person's situation in life is indeed the end-result of human actions, for example, of choices made over a period of time in many different quarters which conspire to grant a measure of good fortune to him or her, or contrariwise to deny access to life's blessings. To say of an illness that it is caused by viral infection, or that hunger and want are the outcome of market forces is to temporise: in the end, a fuller picture is obtained by admitting that human decisions have contributed significantly to the final state of affairs. The mistake of those who feel victimised may be to seek too proximate a person or persons upon whom to lay the blame, but it is understandable that someone weaker or less popular than themselves must make an obvious scapegoat.

It is noteworthy that Niehaus is largely in agreement with Thomas in his social analysis: "Witchcraft accusations clustered in personal relations that were marked by the existence of various forms of inequality. In the vast majority of cases relatively privileged villagers accused those who were relatively disadvantaged of witchcraft." Subordinate persons rarely had the capacity, he says, to do the reverse. He notes the prominent part played by dreams and other "divinatory revelations" in the complex web of evidence, alongside such phenomena as the anomalous appearance of wild animals, deviance such as nakedness from social norms, and the uncritical acceptance of rumours. It is such apparently supernatural disclosures that are held to indicate a liaison with the forces of evil, beyond merely criminal or undesirable behaviour. In this respect the witch has been termed "the standardised nightmare" of society.

A parallel study by A.Ashforth[14] documents patterns of witchcraft in Soweto since 1994. Its increase appears to bear out the thesis that growing inequalities among relatives or neighbours have been conducive to charges of sorcery: "greedy" people seek to eat others - an explanation still proffered in post-colonial Malawi for the greater prosperity of European or Asian communities. Again, AIDS in sub-Saharan Africa was at first attributed to witchcraft, with some magazines actively dissuading their readers from changing their sexual behaviour. Later it became common to blame western powers, accusing them of employing black magic and / or biological warfare to maintain their dominance in the world, as a substitute for direct colonial rule. For example, the president of Namibia, Sam Nujoma, speaking in Geneva in June 2000 described AIDS as a man-made disease aimed at

---

[14] A. Ashforth: *Witchcraft, Violence and Democracy in the new South Africa* (*Cahiers d'Etudes Africains 38, 1998*)

crippling the African peoples, inhibiting their fertility. Such a stance leaves it unclear, of course, whether witch-hunters or drugs are the more relevant response, resulting perhaps in some of the rather unfocused policies within Southern Africa.

What has been the reaction of the churches in South Africa? It appears that "only the ministers of mission *(mainline)* churches discouraged the belief in witches." Thus, a Methodist remarked, "If people are sick, they're sick; if people are dead, they're dead. We must not ask why." But such teachings had, and continue to have, little impact compared with the hugely popular Zionist churches which actively recognise (like medieval Catholicism) the fear of paranormal forces and practise appropriate remedies. Mission and revivalist churches engage in the relief of poverty and in community projects such as income-generating schemes or the construction of water tanks: their theological focus is on moral behaviour and the promise of eternal salvation. By contrast pride of place is given in Zionist churches to the active work of the Holy Spirit, in combating the destructive sources of suffering experienced here and now. Niehaus summarises: "With conversion to Zionist-type churches, marked by this-worldly emphasis on health and a dualistic cosmology, the malevolence of witches was defined in opposition to the benevolence of the Holy Spirit and cognatic [*related*] ancestors. Alternative explanations of misfortune ... were de-emphasised." It seems that it is because these churches directly address the sickness and distress of people that their numbers far exceed those of the more traditional mission churches. While ordained ministers assume responsibility for preaching (with a strong moral tone), for conducting services and for overseeing organisational matters, the prophets in their midst (who are likely to be lay members individually gifted, as they believe, by the Holy Spirit) receive visions and instructions about the causes of afflictions, their prognoses and treatment. The latter often involves fairly dramatic ritual, alongside prayer and the use of tangible symbols such as cloths, strings or papers that have been blessed. Holy water is in frequent evidence too, as an omni-purpose prophylactic. However, the Zionist Christian Church does not instigate witch-hunts, nor any violence against the person: references to the identity of malevolent assailants are usually non-specific.

Malawi Today

When Christian missionaries reached Central Africa in the late 19th century, they reacted strongly against a number of tribal practices, such as witchcraft trials, poison ordeals, spirit possession, and initiation rites. On occasion, one may note, they were suspected of occult powers themselves, and only received into villages after *mwabvi* (poison) tested on hens or goats gave negative results. So too in 1878 Robert Laws' party was told by the Ngoni chief Chikuse, "When you go, take all your spirits with you. Don't leave even one to plague us afterwards." Chikuse did in fact request a Bible, but Laws refused him, on the grounds that he might well treat it as a charm. It took nearly a decade of patient negotiation, preaching a gospel of peace, before the Ngoni were ready to receive the Scottish missionaries; the breakthrough came in 1886, when Christian prayers for rain were answered dramatically! William Johnson (of UMCA[15]) on the opposite shore of Lake Malawi acquired a similar aura when late one night a lion (weakened by the villagers' spear attacks) dropped dead at his feet. Thus in some measure existing magical beliefs facilitated the acceptance of the Christian faith. If these beliefs were subsequently challenged, there was no intention to impose a radically different lifestyle, or to interfere with African customs unnecessarily. Dr. Hine, giving his charge as Anglican bishop in 1899, is not untypical: he envisioned a "church of the people of the land adapting itself to the special circumstances of the race and country in which it exists".

Where real harm or evil existed, however, it was a different matter, although missions alone had limited influence and so relied upon the colonial administration to eliminate what they perceived as either criminal activity (for so it would be judged in Europe) or morally baneful influences. Thus the Witchcraft Act of 1911 came into force, among other things making the *mwabvi* ordeal illegal. Although sometimes animals might be tested in lieu of the suspect, and although those pre-judged as innocent parties were probably given sufficiently large doses to induce vomiting, nevertheless there are reports of many unnecessary deaths, including children (see below, 5.2). There is a Biblical precedent of a kind, however, in Numbers 5.11ff (see below 2.2). One, probably unforeseen, result of the ban led to diviners having more recourse to other techniques, including spirit possession and ancestral guidance. The *vimbuza* dance found in the north was outlawed in 1922, having been described (misleadingly) as "a cult of the devil". But colonial laws, including those which forbade witchcraft accusations (on the "enlightened" grounds that such beliefs were primitive, baseless and repugnant), could only be enforced to a limited degree, and so there was a tacit agreement with chiefs and traditional authorities to maintain a more realistic level of control i.e. to administer "native law and custom".

---

[15] Universities' Mission to Central Africa

Compromises were also reached between particular missions and individual headmen e.g. on issues such as schooling and participation in initiation rites. The danger of repression, as always, was that of driving practices into the bush, as well as erecting barriers of resentment and probably making family or village conflict harder to resolve. One particularly bad year (1933-34) of drought led to a surge of witchcraft eradication activities. After the independent government came to power in 1964, it became possible to prefer charges against supposed witches (in 1969 reverting to the use of traditional courts), and so for their trial and conviction, which theoretically might be the death penalty. This change of policy arose not least, perhaps, as official inaction had been known to lead to mob lynching. However, those wrongly accused are entitled to claim compensation, which has had the effect once again of inducing people to seek revenge covertly. "Witch-finders" are still in business[16], with Likoma Island a centre for such activity - despite its long Anglican tradition, and the location of its cathedral high altar on the exact spot where in 1889 Fr. Chauncey Maples had witnessed and been unable to prevent three "witches" being burnt to death. Today suspected witches are sent from the mainland ports of Nkata Bay or Nkhotakota on the weekly crossings of the Ilala to be tried on the island. On the return trip a white handkerchief signals to the waiting crowd that guilt has been pronounced (and the supposed witch's face marked accordingly): mob violence then takes over, sometimes leading to unchecked, extra-judicial murder. Clergy continue to protest, but not infrequently are then accused of collaborating with witches themselves. It may be worth noting that one of the leading witch-doctors is a former mental patient.

The spread of western ideas and the growth of education have not led to the elimination of "superstition", as the early missionaries and settlers had once hoped. Cultural change has led instead to much uncertainty, with tensions arising between the small-scale life of the traditional past and the macro-scale impact of the outside world. Issues of ownership, land rights, a cash economy, changing roles and expectations, along with huge population increases and now the impact of AIDS, have in fact led to a rise in witchcraft beliefs and the enhanced role of diviners, healers and herbalists (granted official recognition in the 1970's, and currently concerned about the threat to a number of medicinal plants or trees resulting from land degradation), and more generally "power specialists" who bear a variety of other names, even "professor". "Malawi has the famous case of the healer, Billy Goodson

---

[16] One with a remarkable international reputation, *Nchimi* Chikanga Chunda, died in 1993.

Chisupe, who became very popular in 1994 and 1995. He drew much attention in the national and international media as he had claimed to have found a cure for AIDS (named 'Mchape' by the people) revealed to him by his ancestors. Although the Government Health authorities disclaimed the cure as lacking scientific evidence, the set up had an impact as a moral movement to persuade people to change their sexual habits while the official strategy was to promote the use of condoms to prevent AIDS. Chisupe often reminded people that the values he proclaimed were both Christian and ancestral."[17]

The Church need have no quarrel with herbal medicine *per se*, although issues of hygiene and dosage can leave much to be desired: a lot is to be gained by a partnership between the *wazitsamba* (herbalist) and the "orthodox" practitioner. But in so far as the *sing'anga wa ula* (diviner) and the *sing'anga wa mizimu* (spirit medium) reinforce beliefs that sickness is the result of sorcery or retaliation by spirits of the dead, thus accentuating a climate of fear and suspicion, there is bound to be conflict with the Christian message of forgiveness, reconciliation, and the healing of Christ's love. Herbalists too usually claim that their medicines need help from the spirits to be effective; thus, *chizimba* in the form of graveyard soil, crushed bones, or pubic hair may be added to the mix. People may be warned of the dangers of disobeying their instructions; for example, patients must use the right utensils such as a *kape* (small basket) or a *mthiko* (wooden cooking stick), a reminder that there is often a protective element in the simplest of remedies. Positively, however, it should be recognised that traditional healers may be the only accessible source of help and counselling, and frequently have considerable understanding of psychosomatic problems. Very recently it has been realised that they have a role in reducing the spread of HIV; in the Lower Shire valley, for example, there has been a traditional practice of *kupita kufa*, sexual intercourse with a close male relative (brother-in-law) soon after a widow's bereavement, but herbal remedies are now being used to "chase the bad spirits away".

If herbalists have a Christian background, they may carry out their consultations with clients in the presence of a Bible; a usage of ambiguous value since it clearly verges on the magical. Again, Fr. J.C. Chakanza[18] observes that attempts to harmonise initiation practices with church teaching

---

[17] J.C.Chakanza: *Traditional Healers in Malawi (The Lamp 21- Balaka, Malawi, 2000)*

[18] J.C. Chakanza: *Traditional Religion - Dead or Alive? (The Lamp 34 - Balaka, Malawi, 2002)*

have met so far with only limited success. Nor have changes in possession cults fared much better where now hymn singing, Bible reading and prayer are used to induce the medium's trance, even though possession is "not by the usual ancestral spirits, but by spirits of saints and Biblical figures". "With a few exceptions," Chakanza continues, "these emerging spirit mediums are predominantly Christian women, mostly brought up as Roman Catholics. They carry out their healing ministry independently, although still in communion with their churches. The Catholic Church keeps a cautious eye on them, while other denominations have denounced them as operating under the guise of evil spirits." Indeed, the stand-off between the churches and traditional religion has been most pronounced amongst those of Protestant persuasion, including Nkhoma Synod (Presbyterian with strong Calvinist teachings) in the central region of Malawi, and especially some of the more Charismatic churches. Pastor Mwakibinga of the Pentecostal Holiness Church, for example, has described any putative healings as "the tactics of the devil". Excommunication is still frequently applied for a variety of misdemeanours, including recourse to witchdoctors.

Nevertheless, some traditional practitioners are to be found among the ranks of church members, even outside the Catholic Church. Tambulani Nkhata ("Nyagondwe") is a *vimbuza* healer who belongs to the Lutheran Church, and sees intercourse with *mizimu ya wa papi* (ancestral spirits) as a cherished gift from God. The spirits, she claims, communicate to her the cause and treatment of the problem faced by her client: "I dance to diagnose such cases as high blood pressure, fever, epilepsy, madness, pneumonia, venereal diseases, food poisoning and barrenness, and to establish the cause, whether it is sorcery or otherwise... Once I am highly possessed, I am able to discern who the witch is." It is clear that Christians of many different persuasions, as well as other sufferers, consult her – with or without the blessing of their churches.

In the same northern district, among the Tonga people living on the shores of Lake Malawi, it is not only AIDS but also population growth and hence the pressure on fishing stocks that has led to increased cultivation of "occult" practices. Even twenty years ago, there was little rivalry between fishermen, as their catches were abundant and easily found. Now, however, herbal charms are used extensively[19], either to attract the fish or to undo the powerful magic aimed at fishermen by their erstwhile friends or partners. *Nbatawata* are placed on their *akalanje* (floats), especially on the larger nets, to counter

---

[19] Magic to protect property, livestock, crops etc is also more widespread in Malawi than in the past.

bad medicine; on the leading *mtepa* (stick), to render this and the net invisible to the fish; on the *mtawu* (top rope), to keep the fish inside the net. Other charms are used in season, for example, in May and June when *mwera* winds make fishing difficult. All this is done despite the well-known Tonga proverb, "*Urghargha kuti ubaya somba cha kweni ntchilepa ndichu chibaya somba*".[20] On shore there are also suspicions that some fish are not "real", but have been conjured to look like them. These should not be consumed, as that would poison or otherwise trouble the one who eats. So their taste needs to be tested, and the one who caught the fish needs to be observed, to see if he eats them himself. If he refrains from eating elsewhere, it is a sign of his guilt, as it demonstrates how afraid he is that some other person will have bought and cooked his "magic" fish. A few Christian fishermen have taken the courageous step of resorting to prayer rather than charms, with some apparent success. But this cannot be said to have mitigated the rivalry, nor to have increased the fishing stocks, which is perhaps the more urgent problem for the churches to address.[21]

Further south there are abundant tales of witchery too - where, if it is not the sorcery itself that inflicts harm, it is certainly the fear of the sorcerer. The following examples illustrate the pervasive effects of such fears, even where the Christian faith has been long taught and practised. "There were three brothers in our village. One died, leaving a widow. The remaining brothers quarrelled over whose wife she should be. Eventually the elder one gave in, but then put a curse on the younger, threatening to eat his bones. Within hours," the story runs, "this one lost the use of his legs, and seemed to be turning to jelly. The elder brother was sent for, who demanded the sacrifice of a cow to the appropriate local deity. This done, the villagers gnawed the bones and threw them at the jellified younger brother. He recovered instantly." Nor are church members immune: "Two men competed to be choirmaster. Some months later the unsuccessful candidate lay dying and was heard by his son to complain, 'That man is killing me'. The son has therefore vowed not to go to church again until his father's death has been avenged." Or in a third location: "A couple of domineering Christians, a man and his wife, each held an important lay office in their church, letting it be known that no one would ever dethrone them with impunity. As the woman was found on one occasion drunk and disorderly she was removed from being leader of the women's guild. Her replacement, however, died within a few months:

---

[20] "It's the net which kills the fish, not being a crooked person" i.e. skill, not magic.
[21] I am indebted to Mr. Brighton Chipasi of Zomba Theological College for this information.

hence, for fear of further catastrophe, she was then reinstated. When her husband was found subsequently in the same drunken state, no one even contemplated stepping into his shoes."

It is evident therefore that different world-views exist in Malawi[22] today side by side: the one taught by the churches, the other imbibed with one's mother's milk. Attempts to integrate them have been both sporadic and partial. But consistency is perhaps more the concern of the rationalising European mind than of the sub-Saharan African. In seeking help, for example, it has usually been the case that a troubled client will visit a number of diviners until one is found who is plausibly convincing, his findings being judged pragmatically[23]. Likewise, someone suffering an affliction will go wherever relief is to be found (or is affordable): to a western practitioner of medicine, perhaps, but if not, to a herbalist or *sing'anga*. (This is actually no different from some parishioners I knew in England who resorted to faith healers. When I expostulated that they were self-confessed atheists, the reply came, "It's cheaper than private medicine, especially if it works".) As regards people's fears - of failure, barrenness, impotence, or death - it has to be observed that the churches are not succeeding in their attempts to relieve such anxieties. "Magic," as the distinguished White Father Aylward Shorter describes[24] it, "is essentially a form of ritual self-help: 'There is no church of magicians' (Bronislaw Malinowski). When magic is applied to religious or scientific contexts, it results in a deformation of religion in the shape of superstition, or of science in the shape of nostrums or quack medicines."

Excursus: the stance of Islam

Robin Lamburn, a missionary priest in southern Tanzania for many years, has recorded[25] his observations of an African culture strongly permeated by Muslim beliefs – as found also in some of the villages around Lake Malawi. He notes: "The witch and the warlock are abhorrent to African society. Their activities, real or supposed, are the acme of anti-social activities, and no

---

[22] As throughout Africa: a Congolese poet wrote, 'O unhappy Christian / Mass in the morning / Witchdoctor in the evening / Amulet in the pocket / Scapular round the neck'.
[23] A Kimbu (Tanzanian) proverb runs, 'Round the sick person's neck are many charms'.
[24] A. Shorter: *African Culture (Nairobi, 1998)*
[25] R.Lamburn: *From a Missionary's Notebook – the Yao of Tunduru and other essays (Fort Lauderdale, 1991)*

punishment is too severe for such persons. To the Jew and the Christian alike all such abuse of spiritual power is utterly forbidden. Nor would any good Muslim pretend for one moment to defend witchcraft as something lawful. Yet it must be admitted that Islam has not taken its stand with the other two great monotheistic religions in denouncing witchcraft; on the contrary, in some ways it has given the impression that such activities can be approved by Allah. In the Qur'an there are two very short chapters which are called the *mouwvidhetani* or preservative chapters, and it is these which are commonly engraved on amulets." Fr. Lamburn's experience was that the imprecatory verses were often used to harm others, a practice which he describes as "close to witchcraft". He adds: "It has even been held by an Islamist of my acquaintance that the mere fact that a man learns to write Arabic script, and is therefore able to write the imprecatory verses against others, thereby makes him a warlock." An African literate in Arabic script is a person to be feared, having "almost unlimited power" with few daring to oppose his wishes. If *elimu ya ahera* is the first stage to literacy, it is the more advanced *elimu ya dunia* which includes instruction about writing and applying the curses within the Qur'an, and is therefore desired by some Muslim parents as a means of gaining advantage for their offspring.

Post-Modern Society

In the brave new world of science and technology, when mankind has demonstrated its ever-increasing control over the forces of nature, it might be thought that such African stories are a continent apart, and that magicians would be simply those belonging to the Magic Circle, a trade organisation for conjurers and other entertainers, some of whose party tricks might be expected to evolve in sophistication along with technical know-how. The catastrophes of the twentieth century, which need not be detailed here, put an end to such naivety. The promised golden age has not arrived, even for those countries where living standards have increased to levels that might once have been thought unattainable, and a new age of uncertainty has dawned. There are for many in the west no clear answers to life's meaning, and so the individual must do the best he or she can by way of self-help - and any lifeline may be grasped. In the supermarket of religions, different products may suit different people, so the scene is one of ever-shifting loyalties: "mainstream" faiths may have some appeal, but so may the offbeat and the occult. Behind the search there is often an unspoken desperation, as broken hearts look for solace and frustration seeks some glimmer of hope. Where once Max Weber, in analyzing the onward march of Enlightenment rationality, could describe the world as "disenchanted" of both mystery and magic, he might now note a distinct disenchantment too with their supposed replacements.

In the 1970s, as parish priest in England, I found one of my house-bound communicants much in demand. She had somehow acquired a reputation as a fortune-teller, using cards and reading the palms of her visitors' hands. Scarcely a day passed without clients from a radius of twenty miles or more - all of them, she told me, sad people, perhaps sick or divorced, unemployed or lonely, who simply wanted the future to be less unbearable than the past. I was conscious that she was more in demand than the local clergy collectively. Challenged as to how this activity squared with her Christian faith, she assured me that she always ended in prayer, and reminded her visitors that whatever lay ahead was surely in God's hands. But this is not a lay ministry as yet authorised by church authority!

Again, while one might have supposed that astrology would have begun to wither on the vine when Copernicus or Galileo was born, every popular newspaper or magazine today carries its horoscope[26]. Of late too, TV soaps increasingly feature ghosts and psychic phenomena, and clairvoyants have their waiting lists. There was a time when the England football manager had a charismatic lady guru at hand to help his team (just as a wealthy Roman might well have had his own domestic soothsayer), and had the players been more successful who knows how nationally influential she might have become? One recalls that even Nancy Reagan, First Lady of America, would consult the omens or the stars to find propitious days for Ronald her husband (again, rather as Pilate's wife sent word to him about her cautionary dream in Matthew 27.19), and that in Lithuania in 2003 a spiritual healer-cum-clairvoyant, Lena Lolishvili, is an official adviser to the government of Rolandas Paskas. For that matter, old-fashioned seances have never lost their appeal in some quarters, such as among the elderly and the bereaved, for guidance from "the other side".

As for witches, their numbers are now past counting in first world countries, with around half a million websites devoted to their beliefs and activities. They have their own academies as well as their covens; they cater for all tastes and inclinations (e.g. gay and lesbian witches, or those who tattoo themselves with kabbalistic signs); and it is becoming politically correct to provide witch advisers and chaplains to public institutions. A reputable Roman Catholic college of higher education in London has one such

---

[26] I recall also a priest contemporary with me being rebuked by his archdeacon for including such a column in his parish magazine.

on its staff, while it is *de rigueur* for ecumenical spirituality courses to do the same. It is debatable, however, whether these self-styled witches are in quite the same category as those ancient or medieval witches from whom they claim descent. They are part of the New Age movement, perhaps to be likened to neo-Druids, devotees of defunct observances now recreated in the confused search for life's meaning. But the sanitising of witches and their modern respectability does not mean that theirs is no more than a harmless hobby, nor that evil has been wholly eliminated - nor indeed that the true breed is extinct. Newspapers in the west commonly carry advertisements for "services" rendered by psychic practitioners[27], some of whom at another time and in another place would be termed witches: thus, "God gifted psychic [*Sister Linda*] solves impossible problems, removes all bad luck, never fails, results immediately". Or again, "God gifted psychic love specialist [*Carrie Vanderbilt*]", as well as (routinely) solving the impossible, "removes negative obstacles and calls enemies by name, never fails". There is also a frightening story reported to me by a mother newly returned with her baby from a hospital ward. The woman at the adjacent bed (significantly undergoing abortion, often considered one of Wicca's sacraments) had confessed to being a witch whose daily prayer was for the deaths of all new babies. There is no longer any law to restrain her, as private prayer has no official standing in a modern western state, and witch-hunts, as has been noted, were phased out some two hundred years ago. Yet it would be perilous to assume that her prayers are of no effect, and that she ought to be accorded a "right" to conduct what amounts to spiritual terrorism.

The world today has of course its own obsessions, seized upon and promoted by a sensationalist press. The equivalent of satanic power is now more often ascribed to political and social deviants who are publicly accused and condemned. Since every society needs its scapegoats (see below, 3.2), while "witches" in the west are tolerated and would no doubt defend their rights if challenged (using, in the U.K., the Mysticism and Occultism Federation[28] to champion their cause), it is the suspected child-abuser who is

---

[27] Psychic business generally has been booming since the twin towers attack on New York of 2001.

[28] This pressure group makes frequent complaints to the Radio Authority about broadcasts on different channels which it claims are "offensive". In response the Authority has ruled that "divination" is a part of some belief systems and that attacks upon the occult are tantamount to a denigration of what others hold dear. A Cambridge theologian, Dr. Colin Nicholl, has asked about the further implications of this ruling: "since Satanists worship Satan, is it similarly offensive to portray Satan in

the likelier target, regardless at times of any adequate corroborating evidence[29]. In church youth work, following the shocking spate of revelations in Britain, Australia, Ireland and especially the United States, the presumption is now - sadly, but understandably - that volunteers are guilty of warped intention until proved innocent. Likewise in schools, those teachers who offer a comforting shoulder to a child in distress run a serious risk of prosecution: a phenomenon which societies elsewhere, both past and present, would regard with bemusement, possibly even seeing it as a sign of bedevilment. Theologically speaking, the western attempt to create risk-free societies would seem to run counter to God's risky enterprise in his own creative action.

There is indeed much irrationality and crazed behaviour at the present time, in content different from the past, but equivalent in its mood and its contagion. There is, for example, the hysteria irrupting unpredictably in public life. One such occurrence was the mass outbreak of grief across the world, accompanied by extraordinary folk rituals, at the death of Princess Diana in 1997. This was quite unaccountably thought in some episcopal circles to be the English nation's wholesale return to Christian faith! There is undeniably also the clear manifestation of evil, even acts of savage and bizarre criminality, although it must be recognised that psychiatric disturbance and the use of drugs (ironically, PCP or phencyclidim, a popular street hallucinogen dating from the late 1970s, is commonly known as "angel dust") are often bound up with them. In the early part of 2002 the public in Europe was horrified by the ritual killing performed by two German "Satanists", from which it emerged that these number several thousand in that country alone, with comparable figures elsewhere. Some correlation can be established here between such deviant practices and economic deprivation, indicating that aspects of Satanism can be seen as a protest about exclusion from the greater affluence of mainstream society. However, the defence proffered by the men in question that, being entirely subject to Satan's influence, they were not therefore responsible for their actions was rejected by the court[30]. An international conference held in May 2002 seems to have established a certain

---

negative terms?"
[29] There was even one paediatrician attacked during 2001 in Britain by those whose limited command of language took him to be a paedophile.
[30] This has theological relevance for those parts of Africa where demonic possession is sometimes pleaded as an excuse for committing acts of violence. A potentially more plausible alternative is the "genetic defence", a plea of diminished responsibility on account of one's genetic inheritance.

fascination of Satanists for ritual killings of children in sub-Saharan Africa.

A headline in a respected political journal published during this same period proclaimed, "Hell to pay: a boom in paganism is creating new work for the Church": an account of a "terrifying" exorcism in Tuscany, by no means a unique occurrence. Many Anglican and Roman Catholic dioceses have for a couple of decades retained advisers who specialise in exorcisms, and other churches, officially or unofficially, are equally active. Perhaps for this reason mention of the devil and all his works has been retained in the latest liturgies of Christian initiation, where one might otherwise have expected the demythologisers to have held sway. In provision for healing services "prayers[31] for protection and peace" may likewise be found, to be used "where it would be pastorally helpful to pray with those suffering from a sense of disturbance or unrest". There is a range too of so-called deliverance ministries, which probably unwisely (given that church members often need little encouragement to behave judgmentally) have introduced the phenomenon of the "prayer walk"[32] to sniff out disturbed environments believed to be haunted by evil deeds or unhappy memories. Thus, in an age when computer technology is queen of the sciences, and the electronic revolution has changed the face of modern culture, there is still a keen awareness of the strange and inexplicable, apparently defying all rationality and evading the more conventional channels of social regulation. (Not even computers can escape the devil, according to the Rev. Jim Peasboro of Georgia, USA: in his book *The Devil in the Machine* he explains that "any PC built after 1985 has the storage capacity to house an evil spirit".)

All this has recently been commercialised on the grand scale. Alongside boutiques purveying charms, crystals, numerology kits, Tarot cards, aromatherapy and the rest, there is now big business in the form of computer games, fantasy fiction, and Hollywood. The blockbusters have become neo-medieval, in which the answer to danger is no longer to be found in superior

---

[31] For example, "May the cross of the Son of God, which is mightier than all the hordes of hell, and more glorious than all the hosts of heaven, abide with you in your going out and in your coming in. By day and by night, at morning and at evening, at all times and in all places may it protect and defend you. From the wrath of evildoers, from the assaults of evil spirits, from foes visible and invisible, from the snares of the devil, from all passions that beguile the soul and body: may it guard, protect and deliver you."

[32] I once returned from holiday to discover that a neighbouring priest had exorcised my parish church in my absence, claiming that converging ley lines had made it a centre of satanic attraction.

weaponry, nor even in old-fashioned virtues like courage and strength (although these still feature), but in the power of magic. Evil is portrayed at work deploying the darkest arts, and the prevailing assumption is that it can only be defeated by supernatural forces. These books and films are offered in the name of entertainment, but their success lies in appealing to a not quite dormant sense of the occult which was not, as we once thought, finished for good in the Age of Reason. It is, I believe, mistaken to think (as, for example, Dr. David Hope, Archbishop of York, preaching to General Synod in July 2002) that devotees of Harry Potter or of Lord of the Rings are on the threshold of Christian belief, "a world of wonder and mystery" to which they would readily respond if given half a chance: there are also other disturbing forces at work - in need of serious confrontation - not to mention a growing fixation with virtuality at the expense of what is real.

But the churches have engaged as yet relatively little with these New Age ideas and tendencies; one may note the very fact that in bookshops and public libraries the titles on moderately orthodox Christianity are far outnumbered by those on more off-beat "spirituality" and occult interests. People, it seems, "want to know, what works? not, what is true?" in the words of Brendan Walsh, editorial director of the religious publishers DLT; indicating that in the western world the appetite is now for spirituality rather than for religion. Nevertheless, truth is not entirely subjective, and there are, as I hope to explore here, definite "boundaries of belief". So far the main response has been largely in the hands of individual writers and priests, where by contrast, in relation to historic world religions such as Islam or Buddhism, or to other versions of Christianity, much official effort continues to be expended. It is as if what is happening is unremarkable, passing fads and fashions rather than any sea-change, harmless diversions on a bedrock of sound Christian faith that is still assumed to exist. But this begs the question: are we faced in the western world with a serious reversion to paganism?

Excursus: comments of a latter-day witch[33]

"Witchcraft does not rule out any other religion. I think it is a modern version of old, pagan religions, in fact a religion of the natural world. Being a witch means that you practise magic, but there are many different kinds. We worship the divine force through nature. We believe in a duality – a goddess and a god – two forces of nature. A lot of us are healers, using rekki, crystals, complementary medicine of some kind – anything that will help solve

---

[33] Vikki Metcalf of Weymouth

people's problems, that is, their emotional difficulties. We celebrate eight festivals (including Hallowe'en) each year, following the Celtic time system: it is about harmony and balance, and the natural cycle of birth, life, death and rebirth. Most pagans believe in reincarnation of one kind or another. We go to "summerlands" (like heaven) to be reborn.

Witches come from both genders, all age groups and all walks of life. I read tarot cards, which is not fortune telling so much as guidance on how to shape one's life. People will come to me if they have a problem, if they need to sort out their life and make choices. In a way it might be described as counseling. You can show people where they can go if they want to, that they are in control of their lives and that they alone can make the changes.

Rose quartz is one of the most helpful and calming crystals. It is known as the love stone. This is hermatite, very good for depression and relieving stress, although no one knows why. Crystals tend to choose the person, who may feel a tingle in their hands, for instance. Pagans of all sorts tend to be very at peace with themselves; they are not fighting themselves; they have learned to face up to their negative side, and are more rounded people."

Chapter 2

Faith and Falsehood in the Old Testament

Divination in Ancient Israel

There is plenty of evidence in the Old Testament for the practice of divination and soothsaying. In general they are strongly discouraged, even though known elsewhere, as unnecessary for those who believe and trust in the God of Israel. He is the one who will perform wonders for his people and who will reveal to them what they need to know: according to Amos 3.7, "Surely the Lord God does nothing without revealing his secret to his servants the prophets". God can be trusted to watch over his people, so to bypass the chosen channels of his grace and guidance by occult means is a sure sign of faithlessness.

But God does not disclose himself fully: even his most faithful servant Moses approaches him only in a cloud, and his name is enigmatically revealed as "I am who I am" (Ex 3.14). So it can be said, "Truly, thou art a God who hides" (Isa 45.15), and in Deuteronomy 29.29 we read, "The secret things belong to the Lord our God; but the things that are revealed belong to us and to our children for ever." At times, however, messages received must be sealed for a future generation (Isa 8.16).

Hence the prophet Samuel can liken divination to rebellion against God: both amount to a rejection of God's own word (1 Sam 15.23). So in Isaiah 2.6 judgment is pronounced against the house of Jacob "because they are full of diviners from the east and of soothsayers like the Philistines". "You shall have no more soothsayers" warns the prophet Micah, who also seems to classify their activity as among the pathetic alternatives supposedly rivalling God. Best known of all from the earlier days of Israel is the story of Balaam, a prophet or soothsayer of renown, whom the Moabites are prepared to pay for a curse against the people who have "come out of Egypt" (Num 22-24). The text mocks Balaam for his inability to see the angel of the Lord standing in his way (Num 22.21-35), but upholds his integrity as a diviner who speaks only what he is given to say by God. Elsewhere in the Bible (e.g. 2 Pet 2.15, where "a dumb ass spoke with human voice and restrained the prophet's madness" cf Jude 11) he features as the paradigmatic false prophet, who utters pleasing oracles for gain.

There were of course prohibitive laws against the use of occult powers.

Leviticus 19-20 has very firm proscriptions: "You shall not practice augury or witchcraft ... Do not turn to mediums or wizards; do not seek them out, to be defiled by them ... A man or a woman who is a medium or a wizard shall be put to death; they shall be stoned with stones, their blood shall be upon them"[34]. Similar laws existed in some other near-eastern countries such as Assyria, but as in Israel were not wholly effective. Generation after generation there are the same warnings and denunciations, and the well-known visit of Saul to the so-called "witch" of Endor[35] is a reminder that even those in authority might transgress when feeling sufficiently desperate. In earlier days "Saul had put the mediums and the wizards out of the land", but when the licit channels (viz. dreams, Urim [and Thummim], prophetic oracles) for divining God's intentions were denied him, he resorted to forbidden territory. At this time there is no clear indication that divination by illicit means was ineffective; Samuel's shade did after all appear. It was seen rather as defiance against God, which could not but attract punishment from him. So Saul is firmly categorised as God's enemy, compounding his previous offence (vv16-19); the medium herself appears to escape punishment on this occasion, as did those others who in v3 were merely banished.

Nor was Saul the only offender. 1 Kings 17.6, in describing the fall of Samaria, is clear that retribution has overtaken Israel for repeated lapses into idolatry, divination and sorcery, such as were practised among neighbouring nations: "Therefore the Lord was very angry with Israel, and removed them out of his sight" (1 Kings 17.18). In Judah Hezekiah is commended for walking in the ways of the Lord, but his son Manasseh "burned his son as an offering, and practised soothsaying and augury, and dealt with mediums and with wizards" (1 Kings 21.6). In due time Josiah enacted his reforms (1 Kings 23.24) putting away "the mediums and the wizards and the idols and all the abominations that were seen in the land of Judah and in Jerusalem." This was very much the tenor of Deuteronomy 18.9-14 where these "abominable practices" are seen as characteristic of surrounding peoples, and the very reason why at an earlier date they were dispossessed and driven out of Israel's territory. Some of the mediums and wizards may of course have performed multiple roles, including priestly sacrifice, adding weight to the call for centralization of worship. Behind the later proscription of Leviticus 21.1-5,

---

[34] Compare Exodus 22.18, a verse invoked in European witch-hunts, as in 1692 at Salem, Massachusetts.

[35] More accurately a medium, one with power to summon spirits of the dead (1 Sam 28.3-25).

which keeps a priest away from any burial save of his own family, may have been the desire not only to preserve his ritual purity but also to remove the temptation of intercourse with dead spirits. The Deuteronomic writers seem, however, to have reckoned Josiah's actions insufficient to deflect the punishments provoked by Manasseh's wickedness (1 Kings 23.26-27), and Josiah's death at Megiddo was effectively the ending of Judah's independence.

Throughout this period of frequent malpractice the voice of true prophecy was not silent. As well as Samuel, Isaiah and Micah, there is Hosea's withering scorn: "My people inquire of a thing of wood, and their staff gives them oracles" - although we should note (Hos 4.6) that much blame for this attaches to the priests, who have abandoned their proper role. Warnings are also issued to other nations, with a suggestion here that divination is not simply an act of disobedience for the people of Yahweh: it is actually futile whenever and wherever practised. Isaiah's oracle against Egypt (Isa 19.3) seems to relate to a time of social and religious collapse, with its attendant desperation: "The spirit of the Egyptians within them will be emptied out, and I will confound their plans; and they will consult the idols and the sorcerers, and the mediums and the wizards; and I will give over the Egyptians into the hand of a hard master." This period of confusion and disintegration was indeed followed by the invasion of Piankhi around 716 BC. In just the same way, rather more than a century later, Jeremiah tells the demoralised people of Judah that they are clutching at straws in the face of Nebuchadnezzar's threat: "Do not listen to your prophets, your diviners, your dreamers, your soothsayers, or your sorcerers, who are saying to you, 'You shall not serve the king of Babylon.' For it is a lie which they are prophesying to you" (Jer 27.9-10).

By now it has become almost axiomatic that divination is not to be trusted: it is both wrong and foolish. Almost, but not quite! In Ezekiel 21.18ff the prophet's vision is of a signpost set up for the invading Babylonian army. One points to Rabbah, the other to Jerusalem. The king of Babylon uses divination to decide which route to take: "he shakes the arrows, he consults the teraphim, he looks at the [sheep's] liver." All three evidently point him to Jerusalem, whose inhabitants treat it as false divination. With their king Zedekiah they had sworn an oath of allegiance to the Babylonian king, so think themselves safe from attack: but the prophet, aware that this was sworn on God's name (2 Chr 36.13), knows that it has already been broken by Zedekiah's perfidy with Egypt. Hence God's vengeance must proceed, and for once the divination, pronouncing on this occasion God's own verdict, is correct. The Ammonites, thinking that they will now escape, "divine lies" (v29): their fate was sealed when, having first allied themselves with Babylon (2 Kings 24.2), they changed sides (Jer 27.2). And indeed Rabbah fell soon after Jerusalem itself.

Writing somewhat later, Deutero-Isaiah emphasises God's sovereignty in overturning what diviners may predict: "I am the Lord, who made all things, who stretched out the heavens alone, who spread out the earth - who was with me? - who frustrates the omens of liars, and makes fools of diviners ... who confirms the word of his servant and performs the counsel of his messengers" (Isa 44.24-26). This key passage indicates that not only are some diviners pretentious, and some are simply liars seeking to please those who consult them; but even the claims to have perfected technique, so as to have infallible knowledge of what must befall, are fundamentally flawed. God alone made this universe; and his creative powers remain with him, enabling him to direct and influence the current course of events. Only those to whom he has revealed his truth are in a position to declare it. Zechariah 10.1-2 makes precisely the same point: "Ask rain from the Lord" and ask it at the appropriate time, "the season of the spring rain" (i.e. do not make unreasonable requests), but do not imagine any alternative seeking will produce better results or give reliable weather forecasts; "for the teraphim utter nonsense, and the diviners see lies, the dreamers tell false dreams and give empty consolation."

Methods of Divination

Closer attention now needs to be given to the varied methods of foretelling the future. A number of these have already been encountered; some which seem to have been regarded at times as legitimate ways of accessing God's purposes, at least by his chosen agents, and certainly some which were abused by charlatans or were forbidden *tout court*. One or two practices (e.g. the use of Urim and Thummim) fade from view over the span of Israel's history, whereas in the New Testament astrology (Mesopotamian in origin, with a theoretical basis derived from Hellenistic philosophy) makes a brief appearance for the first time (Mt 2.1) - perhaps in post-exilic times having been challenged by the Priestly school restricting astral influence firmly to the inanimate sphere (Gen 1.18, contrasting with man's dominion in v28)?

Urim and Thummim occur in conjunction except in Numbers 27.21 and 1 Samuel 28.6 where Urim alone is mentioned. They are associated exclusively with the priestly / levitical office (as in Ex 28.30, Lev 8.8, Deut 33.8), and were at first a more weighty responsibility than any sacrificial role. They may have been used in making judicial decisions (Ex 22.8-9); but more importantly, when the high priest was asked for guidance from God, as Joshua might inquire of him before deciding upon battle (Num 27.21), evidently one way of responding was to consult these sacred objects attached to, or deposited within, the priestly ephod. They were perhaps used in conjunction with the twelve stones on the breastplate that bore "the names of the sons of Israel" (Ex 28.30), although C. Van Dam[36] is clear that from rabbinic times onwards no one really understood the original practice. According to 1 Samuel 14.41 they functioned as lots that (guided by God's own hand) singled out one option or its opposite. However, Saul was denied an answer before engaging with the Philistines in 1 Samuel 28.6. At the time of Ezra 2.63 (equivalent to Neh 7.65) there was no longer any priest with Urim and Thummim, however desirable that might be. And at the time of the Maccabees an "assembly" has to legitimize Simon's appointment as high priest in the absence of any true prophet at all (1 Macc 14).

Teraphim, usually translated as "household gods" following mentions in Genesis 31.30-35 (Rachel's theft from her father) and 1 Samuel 19.13-16 (Michal's deception), are at times associated with divination (e.g. Ezek 21.21), although there is no clue as to the manner of proceeding. Their condemnation in 2 Kings 23.24 is presumably covered by the Decalogue's prohibition of "other gods" and "graven images" (Ex 20.3-4); although Hosea 3.4 might be taken to be a favourable reference, listing them with other potentially valuable elements of Israelite society. In origin it is likely that they were connected with the cult of ancestors. They may have been clay figures or masks: certainly a good number of terra cotta and bronze statuettes have been unearthed belonging to Canaanite religion.

Necromancy, or consultation of the dead by a medium, is in evidence in the prophetic and legal literature of the 8th to the 6th centuries BC. It clearly corresponded to a popular belief that the dead could still help their living relatives, in particular by revealing things yet to come. Isaiah, who describes the mediums and wizards as "chirping and muttering", inveighs against the practice with the words, "Should not a people consult their God?" (Isa 8.19), and derisively invokes the spectacle of hungry ghosts wandering the earth unable to eat and be satisfied. It can be assumed that, although Saul's session at Endor is the only such episode portrayed, the fierceness of the laws prohibiting necromancy (Lev 19.31; 20.6; 20.27) and prescribing the death

---

[36] Cornelis Van Dam: *The Urim and Thummim – a means of revelation in Israel (New York, 1997)*

penalty for mediums (Deut 18.11) indicates that not only did surrounding tribes follow this practice, but that Israel herself was seriously tainted.

Augury is not described in detail in the Old Testament beyond the mention of hepatoscopy in Ezekiel 21.21. Elsewhere it took different forms such as observing the flight of birds or the drift of smoke from a fire. The entrails of sacrificed animals might also be examined, which seems to be implied in the story of Balaam (Num 23). Generally, it was a question of applying esoteric knowledge to the reading of omens, and in Biblical times was held in fairly low regard. Indeed, Balaam is forced to conclude that God reveals more powerfully through his word than through the analysis of omens (Num 24.1). We may note that it is the Philistines, having captured the ark of God and found that troubles ensued for them (1 Sam 5), who used the simple expedient of a cart with two untrained cows[37] to divine the truth about their misfortunes (1 Sam 6.7-9). Genesis 44.5 refers to Joseph's conversation about a silver drinking cup used as a means of divination (in technical language, libanomancy, for which a little oil was needed), although the context does not necessarily require us to believe that Joseph himself was such a practitioner.

Trial by ordeal is rarely mentioned. There is a stipulation in Numbers 5.26-28 that a wife suspected of unfaithfulness is to drink "the water of bitterness", holy water in an earthen vessel to which dust from the tabernacle floor has been added. The sign of guilt was body swelling accompanied by "bitter pain". Some commentators interpret Moses' insistence that faithless Israelites should drink water with their idolatrous gold ground into it (Ex 32.20) as a similar test.

The casting of lots (sortilege) was not always done in search of divine guidance, but on occasion (drawing up temple rotas in Neh 10.1 and 1 Chr 24-26; distributing land in Num 36.2 and Ezek 47.21-22; allocating garments in Ps 22.18) could be used to achieve an unbiased, or random, outcome; as also presumably in the choice of a scapegoat in Leviticus 15.8. However, even though the casting of lots to find the person responsible for arousing a storm at sea (Jon 1.7) or to find a day favourable to the massacre of Jews (Esth 3.7) are depicted as taking place at non-Jewish hands, it is clear that God's own influence was seen to be very much at work; in the latter case defeating Haman's evil purposes and giving rise to the annual celebration of *Purim*

---

[37] Animals are generally employed to a larger extent in divination in the east, as described, for example, by R.Mistry in his novel *A Fine Balance (London, 1995)* set in India: "Nor did he restrict himself to palmists and astrologers. Seeking stronger drugs, he turned to less orthodox messengers – card-picking doves, chart-reading parrots, communicating cows, diagram-divining snakes."

(derived from *pur*, the lot). As it is expressed in Proverbs 16.33, "The lot is cast into the lap, but the decision is wholly from the Lord." Such a belief clearly undergirds the further comment (Prov 18.18), "The lot puts an end to disputes and decides between powerful contenders." 1 Samuel 10.20-24 describes the lengthy search "by lot", tribe by tribe, family by family, man by man, to discover Saul as God's chosen king - the same process that tracks down the guilty Achan in Joshua 7. It should be noted that the choice of king is carried out here under the prophet Samuel's control, but is set alongside alternative accounts of Saul's election. This anti-monarchical version (v19) could therefore be something of a parody of the earlier story.

The use of arrows seems to be a related practice. It features in Ezekiel 21.21. It has been suggested that a quiver of labelled arrows was shaken, and the arrow that emerged was considered to give divine guidance on the matter under consideration[38]. But there is also the curious story of David and Jonathan in 1 Samuel 20.12-42. For Jonathan to inform David about Saul's state of mind, he could of course have spoken directly to him as in v42, at the pre-arranged venue: yet he chooses to enact his message by means of arrows, which presumably would be taken as divine confirmation i.e. conveying God's own insight into Saul's attitude towards David. There is a similar drama in 2 Kings 13.14-19 where the dying Elisha offers his final prophecy, here to king Joash. In this we touch also upon the "prophetic gesture": more than a dramatisation of his words, it was thought to give his prediction an inevitability (cf Ezekiel 12.1-20; 37.15-28). This has perhaps some kinship with mimetic magic.

Prophetic Inspiration

If knowledge of the future lies anywhere, it must surely be with God. In the Hebrew scriptures those to whom he chooses to reveal it are above all the prophets. A prophet, wrote Philo of Alexandria, is one who "speaks nothing of his own" but resembles an instrument upon which someone else plays. The prophetic state sometimes occurred spontaneously, or it might be induced, for example, by meditation, by music (1 Sam 10.5-6, 2 Kings 3.15) which might well include dancing, or even be assisted by the use of narcotics. But not all prophetic speech was ecstatic, nor was this necessarily considered the hallmark of authenticity, since spokesmen of the Baalim could perform in like manner[39]. Indeed, it is generally only in later prophetic writings (Ezek 8.3;

---

[38] This practice is forbidden in the Qur'an.
[39] Comparison may be made with the ancient Greek oracle at Delphi. The priestess

11.1; Isa 61.1; Zech 7.12; Joel 2.28) that God's Spirit at work in prophecy is noted explicitly. Some earlier prophets (Gad in 2 Sam 24; Micaiah in 1 Kings 22; Isaiah in 2 Kings 19) certainly acted as sober advisers to the king, or on occasion (Nathan in 2 Sam 12; Elijah in 1 Kings 21) confronted the king with his misdeeds. Again, while some prophets were banded together in guilds (even, as 1 Chr 25.1 describes, prophesying "with lyres, harps and cymbals"), perhaps attached to a shrine such as Bethel or Gilgal, or to the royal court itself, but also found on the margins of society, others were solitary figures. Thus, Isaiah had his own disciples in Jerusalem; Elisha, following Elijah who was certainly no establishment figure, was leader of "sons of the prophets"; while Amos disclaimed any such association. It is evident from 1 Kings 20.41 that the prophet's calling might well be marked by special garb, or by physical scars (induced through self-laceration?) or by baldness.

Broadly speaking, it may be said that divination usually addressed private needs and anxieties, using techniques such as those mentioned above; whereas prophecy, especially in the Biblical oracles handed down from the 8th and 7th centuries BC, articulated messages of wider application, recalling the people to their covenant with God and introducing the idea of his retribution which might yet destroy the whole nation, unless they mended their ways. Indeed, the prophet's calling might be wider still. Jeremiah's mission was to be "a prophet to the nations" (Jer 1.5), a fact of which we are reminded at suitable intervals: chapter 25.15-38 describes the fate awaiting "all the nations" and the concluding chapters 46 and onwards contain oracles addressed to Israel's neighbours.

We have, by contrast, little knowledge of what the cult prophets may have said; but they are not mentioned favourably by the men of God whose words are recorded (even if reworked by later generations). The latter certainly saw themselves as champions of God against moral decline and religious infidelity, and the implication is that cult and court prophets had done little to prevent this happening. This of course raises a question of very great importance: the distinction between true and false prophecy.

Moses, according to Exodus 4.1ff, had at the outset felt the need to establish his credentials with the people. In response, God promised that he would be able to reassure them with as many as three miraculous signs.[40] In

---

(the Pythia) may occasionally have been frenzied, but more commonly, according to Herodotus writing in the 5th century BC, she gave coherent answers – usually written down by her attendants – in response to her clients' questions. Plutarch considered that she spoke with her own voice "under the impulse of Apollo".

[40] It may be that the fourth gospel, presenting Jesus as "that prophet" who should

the event, these signs were performed (v30) and the people accepted Moses (v31). Signs continued to accompany Moses; both before Pharaoh, where God's magic proved more powerful than that of "Jannes and Jambres" (2 Tim 3.8), the Egyptian wise men of Exodus 7.8-13; and also on the wilderness journey. Elijah's prayer too was granted, that he should be known as God's prophet (1 Kings 18.36-40): "the fire of the Lord fell, and consumed the burnt offering" (v38). Other miracles associated with him and with his successor Elisha appear, not so much as confirmatory signs of their authority, but rather as acts of divine compassion (see 3.1). It should further be noted that the main challenge to both Moses and Elijah lay not with their co-religionists, but with rival faiths. We do, however, see faithless Israel attempting to use the ark of the covenant (1 Sam 4.1ff) and later the temple itself (Jer 7.4) as if they had magical potency of their own.

As regards these competing voices within Israel's own religion, it was Jeremiah, followed closely by Ezekiel, who fulminated most of all. He had no spectacular signs with which to authenticate his words, except his own integrity in standing firm to the point of extreme suffering (e.g. Jer 38.6). At times, he may even have begun to doubt his own thoughts: "The heart is deceitful above all things, and desperately corrupt" (17.9). But his trust remained in God, who searches the mind and tries the heart (17.10); whereas his opponents, in his view, had no such confidence. They offered falsely comfortable messages, guaranteeing God's protection to the people he had chosen, regardless of their conduct or of any moral requirement. "The prophets say to them, 'You shall not see the sword, nor shall you have famine, but I will give you assured peace in this place.' And the Lord said to me, 'The prophets are prophesying lies in my name; I did not send them, nor did I command them or speak to them. They are prophesying to you a lying vision, worthless divination, and the deceit of their own minds'" (Jer 14.13-14 cf 23.16-17). According to Jeremiah they had not "stood in the council of the Lord" (23.18ff), or they would not have condoned evil. Religion, and its pronouncements, was too familiar an occupation for them, lacking proper reverence for God's awesome majesty: "Am I a God at hand, says the Lord, and not a God afar off?" (23.23). Jeremiah's own proclamation lacked their presumption, and therefore their complacency, regularly bringing down wrath upon himself. His laments on the burden of his calling are frequent; and it was only the protection of Ahikam, son of Shaphan, that saved him on that occasion when death was meted out to Uriah, a prophet of like integrity

---

come, a greater than Moses, draws upon this passage in respect of Jesus' signs, now many more than three.

(26.20-24). On a subsequent occasion he was rescued from the pit by Ebed-melech the Ethiopian (38.7-13).

The Deuteronomic school certainly attempted to be clear on these matters: soothsaying and divination of any kind were ruled out for God's own people; and the presumptuous or false prophet, as well as any speaking in the name of another god, would surely die (Deut 18.19-20). There was indeed a straightforward test of his message: if it did not come about, then it was not a word which God himself had spoken (vv21-22). Unfortunately neither of these assertions allowed easily for empirical verification, as all of us, good and bad alike, are mortal; and if any prediction seems to have failed, it may be that more patience is needed in waiting for its fulfilment. In fact, there are other considerations too; God's word may well be conditional, but semitic idiom prefers the absolute[41]. Hence, a promise as well as a threat may be withdrawn if people's response warrants it. The man of God who addresses Eli in 1 Samuel 2.27ff can thus contrast God's earlier promise (v30) with his change of heart (v31), and later in the same writing God can likewise repent of his choice of Saul as king. There is one further nuance, introduced by Deuteronomy 13.1-3: a prophet's words may actually come about (v2), but must nevertheless be measured carefully against the test of true faith. One who leans towards other gods is not to be heeded (v3), even though his words are accompanied by impressive signs and wonders.

Challenged by Hananiah, also claiming to be a prophet yet preaching an untroubled peace, Jeremiah allows that, if peace is maintained, Hananiah will of course be vindicated (Jer 28.9). There follows a dramatic altercation, as Hananiah breaks Jeremiah's wooden yoke, and the latter announces that in truth the yoke of servitude will be made of unbreakable iron. His prediction of Hananiah's demise comes true shortly afterwards (v17). Similar warnings against falsehood are issued later by Ezekiel, who may well have known some of Jeremiah's oracles, although he uses vivid imagery of his own. In Ezekiel 12.21-28 the prophet faces his critics: there is a proverb going the rounds, "The days grow long, and every vision comes to naught", apparently being used to decry warnings from the past. Ezekiel insists (v23), "The days are at hand." Likewise, the proverb is twisted to apply to what Ezekiel himself proclaims: "He prophesies of times far off", hence his words are irrelevant to those who hear them. Once again his reply (v28) is, "None of my words will be delayed any longer, but the word which I speak will be performed, says the

---

[41] T.E.Lawrence, who lived among Arabs during the 1st World War, reckoned that his desert friends always saw things in black or white, with no half-tones and no shades of grey: "their thoughts were only at ease in extremes."

Lord God." There follows the condemnation of three separate groups of false prophets: those who "who follow their own spirit and who have seen nothing" (Ezek 13.3); those who have misled people by saying "Peace", when there is no peace (v10) - which Ezekiel likens to daubing a wall with whitewash (i.e. incapable of withstanding a storm) - indicating too that such prophets will be forced to acknowledge their lies when they too perish (v14); and lastly, a group not encountered before, women who indulge in divination, apparently issuing protective charms to be worn on the wrist or as a head covering, perhaps in return for barley and pieces of bread (although the details remain obscure), but certainly without demanding any moral reform[42] (v22). Alternatively, it is possible that some kind of sorcery is being described here.

There are just one or two hints in the Hebrew scriptures that God can use even the lying prophets to achieve his purpose. In 1 Kings 22.19-40 Micaiah gives due warning that "the Lord has put a lying spirit in the mouth of all these your prophets", enticing Ahab to a fateful battle with the Syrians. But Micaiah is disbelieved, and even though Ahab took the precaution of disguising himself, he is struck down "according to the word of the Lord which he [Micaiah] had spoken" (v38). Had it not been for the lying prophets, seen here as unwitting agents of divine retribution, Ahab might perhaps have survived. In an earlier incident (1 Kings 13) there is a salutary story of an upright prophet who is foolishly deceived by a lying prophet into breaking the fast imposed upon him by God. His fate is death, but the lion (who is God's agent of punishment) mercifully refrains from eating his body, at which spectacle the lying prophet is moved to repentance. Truly, it might seem, "God moves in a mysterious way / His wonders to perform" (in the words of the 18th century hymnwriter William Cowper)!

Visions

Before the appearance of the prophets, the patriarchs themselves are portrayed as receiving both direct and indirect communication from God about his intended plans. "The word of the Lord," states Genesis 15.1, "came to Abram in a vision." The account that follows of God's covenant pledge seems partly a dream but also something of a wakeful response by Abram i.e. his preparation of the sacrifice. Then, presumably in a vision, he sees passing between the pieces "a smoking fire pot and a flaming torch" (v17), symbols of

---

[42] Gregory the Great applied this passage to bishops of his own day who "cushioned" those in their charge by not correcting their ways. In so doing they no doubt made life easier for themselves - a perennial temptation for church leaders.

God's presence, akin to the pillar and cloud that later led the Israelites to freedom (Num 14.14). Abraham, who interestingly is called *navi*, a prophet, at one point (Gen 20.7, although the connotation here may be that of an intercessor), is shown conversing directly with God in Genesis 18.23. In an equally vivid account later (32.24-32) Jacob is pictured as wrestling with him.

We meet a flame of fire again in Moses' vision of the burning bush (Ex 3.1-6); and when he ascends Mount Sinai (Ex 24.15-18) there the Lord calls him "out of the midst of the cloud" and he sees God's glory "like a devouring fire". In Numbers 12, after what appear to be racist comments against Moses' Cushite wife, we learn how uniquely privileged Moses was considered to be. God appears in a cloud and reminds Aaron and Miriam of their brother's standing: "If there is a prophet among you, I the Lord make myself known to him in a vision, I speak with him in a dream. Not so with my servant Moses; he is entrusted with all my house. With him I speak mouth to mouth, clearly, and not in dark speech; and he beholds the form of the Lord." Other Israelites never saw God's form (Deut 4.15, hence any carved images of God were illicit), but Moses spoke "face to face" (Ex 33.11) - although this is carefully qualified in vv17-23, where the favour granted is to see God's "back". No one, not even Moses, could actually see God's face and live (v20)[43]. The Israelites reckoned it was almost too much to hear his voice: "this great fire will consume us; if we hear the voice of the Lord our God any more, we shall die" (Deut 5.25). The Pentateuch closes with the comment, "There has not arisen a prophet since in Israel like Moses, whom the Lord knew face to face" (Deut 34.10). This is detailed further in Numbers 7.89, where regularly "when Moses went into the tent of meeting to speak with the Lord, he heard the voice speaking to him from above the mercy seat": the verb *meeddabber* is reflexive, suggesting that when Moses entered the tabernacle he found God already speaking, as if to indicate his omnipresent word only needed the right person to listen and to understand.

However, the prophetic writings not infrequently commence with the proclamation that divine messages have been "seen" rather than "heard", although Isaiah 22.14 7
which is emphatic about the prophet's "ears" should also be noted. Thus are recorded "the words of Amos, who was among the shepherds of Tekoa, which he saw ..." (Am 1.1); "the vision of Isaiah" (Isa 1.1) and "the word which

---

[43] "The scriptures do not mean to suggest by this that the vision of God causes the death of those who enjoy it ... On the contrary, God is by nature life-giving" (Gregory of Nyssa: *The Life of Moses*). The point, Gregory explains, is that anyone who thinks he has truly seen (i.e. understood) God is mistaken, and so lacks "life".

Isaiah the son of Amoz saw" (Isa 2.1). Obadiah, Micah, Nahum, and Habakkuk all begin with similar phraseology. And there is that contrasting, and sobering, thought of 1 Samuel 3.1, "The word of the Lord was rare in those days, there was no frequent vision" (noting that Samuel's call is then presented unusually as an "audition"). When God's Spirit falls on Balaam for him to begin his "discourse", it is twice described as "the oracle of the man whose eye is opened, the oracle of him who hears the words of God, who sees the vision of the Almighty, falling down, but having his eyes uncovered" (Num 4.3-4, 15-16). So the test of Elisha's prophetic calling, according to the departing Elijah (2 Kings 2.9-12), is whether he truly "sees" his master being taken up to heaven. There is therefore a possibility that the story of Elijah on Mount Horeb (1 Kings 19.8-13), where God speaks not through the typical accompaniments of a theophany but through a still small voice, is intended to account for the transition to God's self-revelation through the prophetic word, leaving the prophetic vision as an inherited convention[44]. Much later the motif of the prophet's "eye" is prominent in the post-exilic Zechariah, where it occurs some sixteen times (e.g. 4.10, 9.8, 11.17, 12.4). And by now, we may note, the prophet is advised by an angelic intermediary (1.9,11,12,14 etc).

Of course, most of the prophets record a number of imaginative scenes through which God's purposes are revealed. These are "visions" in the more familiar use of the term - as, presumably also, in the missing "visions of Iddo the seer" mentioned in 2 Chronicles 9.29. Visions are described, for example, in Amos 7-9, and famously in Isaiah 6 where the prophet, like Micaiah in 1 Kings 22.19, records "seeing" the Lord sitting on his throne. Visions occupy perhaps one-third of the book of Ezekiel: indeed, there is a single sustained vision that runs from chapter 40 through to the end. Towards the close of the Old Testament period (e.g. Dan, Isa 24-27, Joel 3, Zech 9-14) "pictorial language", in fact the use of apocalyptic imagery, became the normal way to convey divine truth, where the earlier style had made greater use of poetic rhythms suggestive of "divine speech".

This later development may be distinguished from prophecy in more than one way. There is pseudonymity, whereby the author assumes the name of a great personage of the past[45], thereby claiming heightened authority for his

---

[44] R.Davidson in *The Courage to Doubt (London, 1983)* comments: "Elijah does not stand alone at this point in Old Testament tradition. Some of the most hallowed symbols of God's presence with his people, whether verbal or visual, had to be broken so that people might find find God anew."

[45] Pseudonymity in this respect is not dissimilar to the medium's claim to be the

work and effectively making the assertion that what is written has been foretold long ago. There is also the increased use of symbolic language, some of which is accessible to us through familiar Biblical metaphors, but elsewhere employing more obscurely coded references[46]. Then there is too the sense that God's purposes can no longer be achieved wholly within the time-span of history, because what is being endured is part of a climactic battle between the forces of good and evil that can find its complete resolution only on a supra-historical plane. The apocalypse in this way affords encouragement and consolation to those who are facing insuperable odds, such as persecution or even martyrdom, in their earthly struggles. These are now seen as the birth pangs of God's coming new age of peace and justice, when all wrongs will have been righted. Mention is typically made of cosmic aspects of the struggle i.e. a war in heaven in parallel with events on earth, and writers in this idiom often employ similar symbolic sequences.

Although the apocalyptic genre has excited frequent attention down the centuries, its predictive content is limited. Its principal purpose was usually to assure a beleaguered people of God's support and of the reward that their faithfulness would receive in his ultimate victory. If any time scale was suggested, it was of course well known that "with the Lord one day is as a thousand years, and a thousand years as one day" (2 Pet 3.8), or, in the words of the Psalmist, that "a thousand years in thy sight are but as yesterday when it is past, or as a watch in the night" (Ps 90.4). Biblical days are seldom measured by exact timepieces, referring as they do to God's pacing of events which are often seen to be either "very soon" or alternatively "in the fullness of time".

Dreams

There is no clear-cut distinction in the Bible between visions and dreams. Dreams ("night-visions" in Zech 1.8; 4.1; "fancies and visions of my head" in Dan 4.5), one may observe, are however a more commonplace phenomenon. Although they were a respected means of revelation in the ancient world, later writers in the Old Testament were a little cautious about their significance[47].

---

mouthpiece of a departed spirit.

[46] And surely giving rise to doubts about its revelatory value. Austin Farrer once commented, "Revelation not understood is not revelation".

[47] I have never myself experienced a dream which seemed to be signaling a message of any great moment. Nevertheless I am very aware of a related phenomenon – the activity of the unconscious mind. In the days when I wrestled with mathematical

"A hungry man dreams he is eating", "a thirsty man dreams he is drinking" (Isa 29.8) - but alas! when they awake it is but an illusion. In Ecclesiastes 5.3 there is the recognition that "a dream comes with much business" - what would today be called "anxiety" dreams. Of course, people are equally anxious to learn if any meaning attaches to them, so v7 comments, "when dreams increase, empty words grow many", most of which Qoheleth seems to think are unhelpful and distracting: "but do you fear God", he adds.

Most dreams "fly away" (Job 20.8), or, if the terrors of the night are still half-remembered, "on awaking you despise their phantoms" (Ps 73.20). Yet Job 33.14ff is insistent that God can, when men are in a deep sleep, open their ears and terrify them with warnings; as also he can use the trials of pain and suffering (v19) to do the same. Eliphaz (Job 4.12-17) reports on such an experience to Job, when "dread came upon him, and trembling", and a hair-raising spirit actually spoke to him.

In Sirach 34 there is a somewhat lengthier discussion. "Dreams give wings to a fool's fancy. Paying heed to dreams is like clutching a shadow or chasing the wind. What you see in a dream is nothing but a reflection … Divination, omens, and dreams are all futile, mere fantasies … Unless they are sent by intervention from the Most High, pay no attention to them. Dreams have led many astray and disappointed those who built their hopes on them. The law is perfect without such illusions." In this assessment, which allows for the exceptional revelatory experience, he is not so far from the position of the Deuteronomists, and indeed Jeremiah, centuries earlier. A "dreamer of dreams" (Deut 13.1-5) is not usually to be trusted, teaching rebellion against God, whose laws are both accessible and sufficient (30.11-14). So revelatory dreams are generally unnecessary. There is a similar attack upon "lying dreams" in Jeremiah 23.32 and 27.9, as later in Zechariah 10.2. Jeremiah does report one refreshing dream of his own, however. After hearing a promise of Judah's future restoration, he comments, "Thereupon I awoke and looked, and my sleep was pleasant to me" (Jer 31.26).

But another strand in Biblical tradition was altogether more confident in dreams as a medium for divine communication. It was accepted (e.g. Num 12.6) that God might speak with prophets in this way, even if at times somewhat darkly or enigmatically (v8). Shrines where God's presence was known were particularly suitable places for this to happen: Jacob's famous

---

problems, I frequently fell asleep with a problem unresolved; then after an untroubled night would at once on waking know the solution that had evaded me the previous evening. The mathematician Alfred North Whitehead found the same, and recent research at Harvard Medical School corroborates the experience.

dream occurred at Bethel (Gen 28.10-22), and in 1 Kings 3.4-15 it was at Gibeon where "the Lord appeared to Solomon in a dream by night". But God could even address Abimelech, the foreign king of Gerar, with a dire warning about Abraham's wife Sarah (Gen 20.1-7) - and it is also foreign kings and their dreams who feature later in the Biblical accounts.

What is clear in this tradition is that dreams need proper interpretation, if God's message is to be heard[48]. It is of course Joseph and Daniel who are renowned in this respect. Joseph was a dreamer himself (Gen 37.5ff) and recounted his dreams in such a way that their meaning was unambiguously, and even objectionably, plain. Subsequently in prison in Egypt he has the opportunity to use his God-given gift (Gen 40.8), which two years later stands him in good stead with Pharaoh (Gen 41.12ff). He had the ability to see the pattern of events in the symbols of the various dreams, unlike "the magicians of Egypt and all its wise men" (v8). There is a rabbinic saying, "All dreams follow the mouth" (and rabbinic writers were seldom dismissive of dreams), which suggests that it is the interpretation of a dream that has the power to bring it about. This is evident with Pharaoh's dreams, as with the dream and its explanation overheard by Gideon in Judges 7.13-15.

As for the book of Daniel, composed much closer to the time of ben Sira, its hero is also both dreamer (Dan 7.1ff, where he prudently records his vision) and interpreter (1.17; 2.16, 24). Here the exercise is intensified by the refusal of Nebuchadnezzar to disclose his dream, which not unreasonably his own magicians, enchanters, sorcerers and Chaldeans request of him. But after prayer "the mystery was revealed to Daniel in a vision of the night" (2.19). He loses no opportunity for testifying to the greatness of Israel's God. "There is a God in heaven who reveals mysteries" (2.28 cf 2.44-47), contrasting strongly with the ineffective gods known to the wise men of Babylon. The word "mystery" used here embraces rather more than the mere details of Nebuchadnezzar's dream. Whereas earlier prophets could focus their message upon God's immediate requirements, now history is seen as more complex. The divine plan behind it is more elaborate, and indeed mysterious, but still accessible to his chosen servants.

"To interpret a dream", as in Daniel 4.6, is in Akkadian *pasaru*, and from this is derived the technical term *pesher*, which from the late 1st century BC became a growing industry in early Judaism. The Qumran Pesharists are the earliest representatives of this genre, which can be described as "fulfilment exegesis". The material on which they worked was not dreams so much as

---

[48] In this may be noted a similarity with Paul's views on glossolalia in 1 Corinthians 14. Interpretation is essential, and is a valued gift of the Holy Spirit (1 Cor 12.10).

biblical texts and prophecies, now regarded as a code which when deciphered would predict events in their own day. For them, as for the apocalyptic writers (but unlike ben Sira), the law needed to be supplemented with contemporary revelation: the one group preferred new visions using imagery drawn from the past, the Pesharists believed that there was more truth to be uncovered in familiar texts. It was axiomatic for them, and appears to have been already understood in this way in Zechariah 1.4-6, that all prophecy was a unity, holding the key to present circumstances.

We may reflect that even though the Christian church at its inception might rejoice in the advent of a new divine initiative, leading to the fulfilment of Joel 2.28 ("your sons and your daughters shall prophesy, your old men shall dream dreams, and your young men shall see visions"), in due course it too would find itself challenged by similar issues, needing to articulate its position on such matters as: scriptural teaching from the past; God's revelation in Christ; its own canon of scripture; the continuation of divine guidance; the needful source of authority to distinguish truth from falsehood.

Malpractices

Although the activity of witches and sorcerers is clearly condemned in the Old Testament (e.g. Ex 22.18), it is by no means clear what practices are being referred to, beyond the arts of divination and necromancy. The "harlotries and sorceries" of Jezebel are verbally attacked in 2 Kings 9.22, but the main accusation against her (1 Kings 18.19) is that she encouraged the worship of Baal, the Canaanite rain god, and of Asherah, the mother goddess popularly considered as Yahweh's spouse. It hardly seems that overmuch support was needed, as these rival cults, and that too of Astarte, the Canaanite / Sidonian fertility goddess, presumably thought to bring more immediate benefits to their devotees, seem to have flourished alongside or instead of the worship of Yahweh over long periods of time anyway (Judg 2.11-13; 1 Chr 8.33-34; 14.6; 1 Kings 11.5,33; Jer 7.18). The high god of Canaan, known as El Elyon, El Shaddai, El Olam in Genesis 14.22; 17.1; 21.33 respectively, was by contrast frequently identified with Yahweh. The Deuteronomic stipulation against exogamy (Deut 7.1-6) was still needed in the 7th century BC to guard against the continuing and ever-present danger of apostasy. Jezebel was also guilty of inciting king Ahab to injustice and murder (1 Kings 21.5ff, 25-26). 2 Kings 9.30 mentions her cosmetic habits, which may give another aspect of her "harlotry" but were hardly related to any sorcery. Likewise Malachi 3.5 is unspecific about sorcery, ranked alongside adultery, injustice and brutality.

Some commentators see Psalm 64.3, the aiming of "bitter words like arrows", as referring to malevolent spells, but the context seems to suggest more straightforwardly that these were malicious plans. There is a term normally translated "evil-doer", occurring in some thirteen psalms (e.g. 5.5; 6.8 ...) which Mowinckel argued should be read instead as "sorcerer". His proposal was that the sickness that had overtaken the Psalmist was the result of being cursed. But even the language used in Psalm 41.8, "a deadly thing has fastened upon him", may be understood as no more than the account of a wasting illness, which insincere friends hope will soon be fatal. Mowinckel's interpretation nonetheless cannot be ruled out. If accepted, the proposal that Psalm 140 is a counter-curse would have some plausibility: "let the mischief of their lips overwhelm them, let burning coals fall upon them" (vv9-10). But there are of course psalms that, in asking for God's help, call for the thwarting of evil and the destruction either of one's personal foes or of Israel's enemies (e.g. 55, 109, 129, 137).

There are in fact very few individuals in the Old Testament recorded as uttering curses (even if one counts Jeremiah and Job each cursing the day that he was born). The prophets, by contrast, issue many warnings (e.g. Am 5.11, Hos 4.10, Jer 17.13, Zech 5.14), but these are addressed to God's people generally, within the context of their covenant with Yahweh. This is indeed the Deuteronomic framework too, as spelled out clearly in Deuteronomy 11.26ff and 28.15ff (cf Jer 11.1-3, also Lev 26.14-39). The various warnings were understood as being fulfilled with Judah's Babylonian captivity, although God's own curse was effective at any time against particular persons (Gen 4.11, Deut 27.15-26, Prov 3.33, 1 Kings 16.34 cf Josh 6.26) or against those who neglected their religious duty (Hag 1.6; 2.17). The story of Balaam is important theologically in its indication that curses could not be pronounced, or would certainly not be effective, if they ran counter to God's will; a point that is made also in Proverbs 26.2, "a curse that is causeless does not alight". So when Shimei curses king David in 2 Samuel 16.5ff, we learn that David forbids his silencing, recognising that he is God's mouthpiece (vv10-12). Cursing as an activity, if not done at God's behest, is an empty outburst that will draw down its own punishment. Cursing one's own parents was regarded as particularly heinous (Ex 21.17).

There are just a few other specific practices that were forbidden:-
- Cooking a kid in its mother's milk (Ex 23.19): a text from Ras Shamra indicates that this might have been part of an agricultural fertility rite, with the product sprinkled on a field.
- Trimming the edges of one's hair, cutting into one's flesh or tattooing, on

account of the dead (Lev 19.29-30): perhaps this was done in the hope of maintaining some life in dead spirits.
- Child sacrifice, usually by fire (Lev 20.1-5; 2 Kings 3.27; 16.3; 17.17,31; 21.6; 2 Chr 33.6; Jer 7.31; 19.5): the particular site associated with this was Topheth, to the south-west of Jerusalem. The offering may have been to Baal, as Jeremiah suggests, or to Molech, if that was indeed the name of a god (cf Acts 7.43), or to "demons" (Ps 106.37). Topheth was destroyed by Josiah in his Yahwistic reforms (2 Kings 23.10).

The indication is that all of these were vestiges of Canaanite religion continuing to coexist with the worship of Yahweh.

In the earlier days of Israel's history, the main response to religious infidelity which such practices constituted was that of simple condemnation. Latterly, however, ridicule came to be employed as well. It may be seen in the description of Elijah's confrontation with the prophets of Baal. "At noon Elijah mocked them, saying, 'Cry aloud, for he is a god; either he is musing, or he has gone aside, or he is on a journey, or perhaps he is asleep and must be awakened'" (1 Kings 18.27). Deutero-Isaiah is also a master in this field. After an idol has been fashioned, he says, "they set it in its place, and it stands there; it cannot move from its place - if one cries to it, it does not answer or save him from his trouble" (Isa 46.7). Or again he mocks the magicians and diviners, "Stand fast in your enchantments and your many sorceries ... perhaps you may be able to succeed, perhaps you may inspire terror ... let them stand forth and save you, those who divide the heavens, who gaze at the stars, who at the new moons predict what shall befall you" (Isa 47.12-13).

It is worth recording too, from a much later period, the sophisticated rationalism of "Daniel, Bel and the Snake". This writing dates from around 100 BC, and appears in the LXX (Septuagint) as an addition to the book of Daniel. Bel is the same Baal as before, but his worship is exposed as a hoax when Daniel manages to record the priests' footprints on the floor of the temple by sprinkling dust, thus proving that it was they and their families, not Bel himself, who ate the food offerings. Irenaeus was the first church father to display knowledge of this composition, which surely deserves wider circulation today. The gullible still need protection against quacks and charlatans, who may be found in any walk of life and in any religion or culture. While ridicule is a weapon to be used perhaps sparingly, the unveiling of fraud and falsity is surely never inappropriate.

Chapter 3

Life's Uncertainties in Hebrew Perspective

Sickness and Suffering

Examples have already been noted of how, at times of stress or danger, recourse is made to any practitioners who it is thought may offer a way out, or at the very least provide some assurance about the future. The perspective of the Hebrew Bible is that all things lie in the hands of God, and that therefore he alone can properly determine the outcome of events. To bypass his chosen instruments for making known his will and purpose was deeply unacceptable. Equally, to frustrate his plans by summoning other powers, whether earthly or supernatural, to one's aid was rebellion against him. What then of sickness, or other forms of distress? How far were they seen as of human or of divine origin? What was the sufferer, or victim, to make of them? Were there legitimate avenues for healing and recovery? Could sacrifices make any difference?

Certainly it is not surprising to find many places where sickness and suffering are considered to be the result of incurring divine displeasure. There are frequent warnings in Deuteronomy: those who love God and keep his commandments will be blessed with good health (7.15); whereas God "will not be slack with him who hates him, he will requite him to his face" (7.10). This latter possibility is spelt out in great detail in chapter 28: consumption and fever are mentioned (v22), as are the boils of Egypt, ulcers, scurvy, the itch, madness, blindness, and confusion of mind (vv27-28). This is quite apart from drought, pestilence and defeat in battle, and a multitude of unspecified troubles also to be expected (v61). Leviticus 26.14-39 is equally devastating in its description of the consequences of unfaithfulness: terror, fever, plague, starvation and utter desolation will certainly ensue, although a people who turn back to God will be spared the more extreme disasters. The essential conditions for regaining God's care and protection are spelt out in vv40-41: confession, humility and the making of reparation.

These general admonitions were seen as fulfilled in the time of Judah's exile. But long before then many different individuals sinned and suffered the consequences (and of course God could visit his wrath upon people anywhere and at any time, as he did with the Flood and with the plagues of Egypt, just as at other times punishment might be deferred or even apparently cancelled[49]). Saul's evil spirit is sent "from the Lord" in 1 Samuel 16.14 following his disobedience. Later his successor David sins with Bathsheba, and so "the Lord struck the child that Uriah's wife bore to David, and it became sick", dying a few days later (2 Sam 12.15-18). Skin diseases affect Miriam (Num 12.9-10) and also Uzziah (2 Chr 26.19) for their arrogance towards God. Notorious sinners could be considered "blotted out of the book of the living" (Ps 69.28 cf Ex 32.32; Mal 3.16; and see 4.3 below). On the wider front (outside Israel) tumours are inflicted upon the people of Ashdod, so long as they hold the Ark of the Covenant in their possession (1 Sam 5.6). Thousands perish too in the Assyrian army which dares to threaten Jerusalem (Isa 37.35-36).

Suffering was not necessarily, however, the consequence of sin. In the first place, death is universal. And while it may have been introduced into the world by Adam's fault (Gen 2.17), it was not always seen as personal punishment, nor were the conditions which led to it. Exodus 20.5 states that "the iniquity of the fathers" may be visited "upon the children to the third and fourth generations of those who hate me". But this is realism about the long-lasting repercussions of foolish or evil behaviour: children and grandchildren may be the victims of wrongs they have not themselves committed. For his part (and with less realism), Ezekiel insists upon personal responsibility. His watchword is "the soul that sins shall die" (Ezek 18.4,20). He overturns the old proverb, "The fathers have eaten sour grapes, and the children's teeth are set on edge": "As I live, says the Lord God, this proverb shall be no more used by you in Israel" (18.2-3). Solomon's prayer of 1 Kings 8.37-39 was an earlier plea for divine justice: "hear thou in heaven thy dwelling place, and forgive, and act, and render to each whose heart thou knowest, according to all his ways."

In the second place, there are examples of sickness or death which appear quite "unmerited". In the Elisha stories of 2 Kings, the Shunammite's son dies suddenly, despite the fact that his birth was apparently gifted by God as a reward for the parents' hospitality towards "the holy man of God" (4.8ff); a story very similar to that of 1 Kings 17.8-24 featuring Elijah and the widow of Zarephath. Later there is Naaman, whose battle triumphs were a sign of God's favour: yet he subsequently contracted leprosy (5.1ff). Best known of

---

[49] Manasseh was a test case: 2 Kings 21 describes his many abominations, yet he lived peacefully and died at a good age, after reigning for 55 years. 2 Chronicles 33 therefore made an attempt to rehabilitate him, as did the later Prayer of Manasseh. Rabbinic sources (cf Apocalypse of Baruch) debated whether he had any place in the world to come.

all is Job, "blameless and upright, one who feared God, and turned away from evil" (Job 1.1). His afflictions, which were many and severe, are portrayed as a test of his faith, permitted by God. Job's comforters relentlessly propose conventional wisdom. Eliphaz, for example, advises how happy should be "the man whom God reproves" (5.17); after being chastened, he will find that the Almighty's hands then bind up and heal. But Job himself denies transgression, as in the end he eschews any simple explanation: it is a mystery lying in God's hands (42.3). The pietism of Psalm 91.9-10, "because you have made the Lord your refuge ... no evil shall befall you", is - at least in some later Hebrew writings - subjected to close questioning. Qoheleth finds that "time and chance" have a large part to play (Eccl 9.11). There is less justice on earth than we like to imagine: "I saw all the oppressions that are practised under the sun. And behold, the tears of the oppressed, and they had no one to comfort them!" (4.1). The psalmist finds himself almost in agreement when he sees the unchecked arrogance of the wicked (Ps 73.2-14): but then, visiting God's sanctuary (v17), his faith is restored. He is reassured that God's justice will prevail (vv18-19), acknowledging his own lack of understanding (vv21-22). Above all he now recognises God's presence as his consolation, in both the present and the future (vv23-24): "God is the strength of my heart and my portion for ever" (v26). In the story of Cain and Abel (Gen 4.1ff) the apparent injustice initially meted out to Cain, whose offering is rejected, leaves him with a challenge: how will he react? "If you do not do well, sin is couching at the door; its desire is for you, but you must master it" (v7): indeed, life is seldom fair, but to be human is to rise above circumstances, however unfavourable.

If there is deeper meaning to be found anywhere in apparently undeserved tribulation, it is surely with Isaiah's suffering servant: "he has borne our griefs and carried our sorrows, yet we esteemed him stricken, smitten by God and afflicted" (Isa 53.4). Hence he concludes: "upon him was the chastisement that made us whole" (v5); an appreciation of desolation that turns whatever is experienced passively, as the consequence of evil in the world around us, into vicarious acceptance of all its pain. Such a reckoning necessarily allows that there is not always an immediate cure for sickness. It may have to be endured, if not for one's own sins, at least for the sake of others. At the very least it may allow one to empathise with others in their suffering, and promote compassion.

What God metes out, he can, if he chooses, withdraw; and where he punishes, he can also forgive and heal. "I kill and I make alive; I wound and I heal" (Deut 32.39 cf Job 5.18). Just as the Old Testament sees God as the author of our just deserts, so he too is the source of both physical and spiritual recovery. Indeed the ancient creed in Exodus 34.6-7 stresses God's "steadfast love" and forgiving nature before ever it warns of his wrath. This is viewed with caution in earlier teachings, in case morality was thereby undermined. But it did call for God's people to exercise charity towards the marginalized, including the deaf and the blind (e.g. Lev 19.9-10,14 and Deut 24.17-22), remembering how they themselves were redeemed from slavery in Egypt. It is after the exile that we find the theme restated, as in Nehemiah 9.17 (cf Ps 86.15; Joel 2.13), "Thou art a God ready to forgive". Indeed, had not Jeremiah envisioned a remnant whom God would pardon (50.20)[50]? Jonah also cited the ancient creed (4.2), but his prejudiced mistake was to magnify God's wrath at the expense of his mercy.

Hence the psalmist could praise God: "Bless the Lord, O my soul, and forget not all his benefits, who forgives all your iniquity, who heals all your diseases" (Ps 103.2-3). It is therefore God to whom the sick must turn, as exemplified in Psalm 38; prayer was no doubt the most common legitimate option available to one who suffered. Ahaziah's fall from an upper window (2 Kings 1.2) is not portrayed as anything more than an accident, whereas his fatal error - i.e. his sin, leading to Elijah's denunciation - was that he looked for an oracle from "Baal-zebub, the god of Ekron". By contrast when the intercession of God's prophet is sought, examples of healing are recorded. Thus, Jeroboam's hand is restored in 1 Kings 13.6, and Isaiah (38.5ff) assures king Hezekiah that his prayer has been heard and his tears noted, with fifteen years added by God to his lifespan. Fearing the Lord, according to Proverbs 3.8, "will be healing to your flesh and refreshment to your bones". And Psalm 41 adds that considering the poor is likely to win God's favour: such a man will be sustained on his sickbed and healed of all his infirmities (v3). The reference in Ezekiel 30.21 to the use of a bandage binding up a broken arm indicates the expectation that those favoured by God would indeed find him mending human infirmities – but in his own good time.

What use then were other possible treatments? King Asa (2 Chr 16.12) had a severe disease "in his feet" (possibly a Hebrew euphemism for his sexual organs). "Yet even in his disease he did not seek the Lord, but sought help from physicians" - and so he perished. Physicians are mentioned as being in Egypt at the time of Joseph (Gen 50.2), a venerable tradition there as in Greece. Indeed, Moses' bronze serpent of Numbers 21.8-9 was probably an Egyptian homeopathic remedy against snakebite; it was later worshipped as

---

[50] Compare the remnant "chosen by grace" (i.e. not according to their deserts) in Romans 11.5.

"Nehushtan" (2 Kings 18.4) and so destroyed by Hezekiah. Wisdom 16.6-7 offers an orthodox theological justification, seeing the serpent merely as "a symbol of salvation". In Israel the estimation of therapies other than prayer, and the reputation of physicians, was generally low. Jeremiah is aware of the presence in Gilead of "balm" (8.22) but points to the uselessness of "many medicines" (46.11); while Job (13.4) describes his friends as "worthless physicians". Yet herbal knowledge was not wholly despised, as can be seen in Hezekiah's case above. Having spoken to God, Isaiah also took the prudent step of applying a poultice of figs to the infected skin (2 Kings 20.7), and he mentions elsewhere the use of oil to "soften" wounds (Isa 1.6)[51]. Elisha too was evidently a man with some botanical lore. In 2 Kings 4.38ff, after his servant had made "a pot of pottage" from wild gourds (perhaps pumpkins?), it was suspected of being toxic. So the prophet lowered the concentration of the concoction by adding flour. With mandrakes, used in Genesis 30.14ff in an attempt to relieve Rachel's infertility, we are on the borderlands between herbal lore and sympathetic magic, for the roots of a mandrake were sometimes considered to resemble the human form. In the early 2nd century BC writing Tobit, fish gall (noted by Pliny as effective in treating scars) is applied successfully to the old man's eyes, removing white patches from them. Here his son Tobias is portrayed as following out angelic instructions.

There was indeed a tradition, going back at least to Solomon[52] (1 Kings 4.29-34), of "wisdom" concerning itself, not only with matters of right behaviour, but also with properties of the natural world. Thus Solomon "spoke of trees, from the cedar that is in Lebanon to the hyssop that grows out of the wall; he spoke also of beasts, and of birds, and of reptiles, and of fish." No doubt some ethical insights could be gained from such observation (as in Prov 30.24-31), and Christ himself could subsequently use such examples to illustrate deep truths about God's kingdom (e.g. Mt 6.25-34; Mk 4.26-32). But there were practical applications too. Proverbs 8.22ff takes a rather different view from Job. The latter confessed that there were "things too

---

[51] Anointing with oil was also used in confirmation of a leper's cleansing (Lev 14.10-32). It is commended for Christian usage in Mark 6.13 and James 5.14-15.
[52] An even older tradition is found in ancient Egypt. The scarab, or dung-beetle, was observed pushing and then burying a ball of dung, which subsequently came to life with offspring. This was seen as a symbol of the sungod Re, who moved across the sky and was then reborn the following day. So effigies of Re have scarab heads, and before being mummified some corpses had their hearts replaced with scarabs to assist their reincarnation.

wonderful" for him (Job 42.3), whereas the teachers of wisdom rejoiced that God's own knowledge and skill had been made, at least partly, accessible to men. It is above all ben Sira, perhaps to counter the more negative assessments, who celebrates "the services of a doctor" (Sir 38.1) and proposes what seems a judicious synthesis: "his skill comes from the Most High" (v2), utilising remedies that the Lord has created from the earth (v4). "A sensible man will not disparage them" (v4), the Biblical example of Moses sweetening the water with a particular wood (Ex 15.25) being cited. So God's healing power is mediated through the work of the pharmacist (v8), whose mixtures give relief from pain (v7). At the same time ben Sira urges both prayer and sacrifice (vv9-11), since the heart too needs cleansing from sin (v10). Nor can the doctor work unaided: he must needs pray to the Lord "to grant success in relieving pain and finding a cure to save the patient's life" (v14). The reading of v15 is a little obscure, but seems to suggest that the doctor's skill cannot be presumed, hence the ill consequences of wilful ways may not always be cured (even though, as Jer 9.1 depicts him, God weeps over his people's sins).

It is ben Sira too who is aware of the interaction of mind and body. "Envy and anger shorten life, and anxiety brings premature old age" (Sir 30.24), while one afflicted by the Lord will certainly have little appetite (30.19-20). It is also true, he advises, that "the moderate eater enjoys healthy sleep" (31.20). So a measure of restraint in all things is best: "in all you do avoid extremes, and no illness will come your way" (31.22). Similar counsel can be found in Proverbs. Thus, "a cheerful heart is a good medicine, but a downcast spirit dries up the bones" (17.22 cf 12.25; 15.30; 16.24), and also "hope deferred makes the heart sick, but a desire fulfilled is a tree of life" (13.12). Implicit in such teaching is that sickness or trouble can often be the intrinsic result of one's own behaviour or of one's attitudes. It need not necessarily be seen as punishment or retribution imposed perhaps rather arbitrarily by God's avenging wrath.

However, rationality never wholly prevails, and alongside this wisdom literature it is clear that in the later years of Second Temple Judaism more primitive fears continued to resurface. In particular, there was a widespread belief (known, for example, also in Babylon) that demons, often in the form of animals, were responsible among other things for much sickness. There is some apparent reference in older texts to such fears: Psalm 106 is explicit about child sacrifice to "demons" (although this may refer to pagan gods, as may the reference in Baruch 4.7), and similar abominable practices are mentioned in Deuteronomy 32.16-17. Psalm 55.9-10 may refer to demons going around the city walls "day and night" causing mischief and trouble, while in Psalm 22.12,16,21 the graphic description of the evildoers as hostile bulls, dogs and lions may, as in Babylonian sources, include demonic powers as well. Indeed Leviticus 17.7 refers specifically to satyrs i.e. demons appearing as goats, forbidding the offering of any sacrifice to them. The horrific description of the Lord's "day of vengeance" in Isaiah 34 (cf 13.21-22) suggests a nightmare scenario in which a desolate landscape is occupied by every sort of demon, including satyrs and Lilith[53] (v14), the latter being an aggressive female demon prone to attack pregnant women and new-born babies. They operated, however, with God's permission (cf his despatch of an evil spirit in Judges 9.23). In the story of Tobias mentioned above, the demon Asmodaeus has already killed seven husbands given to Sarah. But the heart and liver of a fish could be used "as a fumigation for any man or woman attacked by a demon or evil spirit" (Tob 6.7), and indeed it was this smell that drove Asmodaeus back to Egypt, evidently regarded as the home of all demons (8.3). Exorcism in some shape or form was not considered the only possible remedy though. Prayer, repentance and sacrifice (as with Sirach) might all have a part to play, since the demons' defeat was seen to lie ultimately with God.

The Role of Ritual

Although the practice of medicine has always been pursued more thoroughly in some countries than in others, few practitioners would wish to claim too much for its benefits. Hippocrates, who taught and worked on the Greek island of Kos in the 5th century BC, wrote: "In fact, although physicians take many things in hand, many diseases are also overcome for them spontaneously ... The gods are the real physicians." There are, of course, surgical techniques which help to preserve life and drugs which relieve pain and promote healing. Many of these are better understand now than in times past - but not entirely. There also remain ailments and diseases for which there is as yet no cure and sometimes very little relief, despite the expectations of those in consumer-led societies that a course of medication or other treatment must invariably be made available. Hippocrates was nearer the truth in his appreciation that the human body has within itself certain powers of recuperation, which may be assisted to greater or lesser degree by the physician's art. So-called "alternative" therapists are sometimes more in touch with this reality than "orthodox" practitioners. In many countries there

---

[53] Lilith is wrongly translated as "night hag" in RSV.

is in fact a growing dialogue and an exchange of knowledge between the different schools of healing.

In particular, there is a growing awareness of ben Sira's insight mentioned above: the interaction of mind and body, what Keith Thomas described (see 1.3) as "the therapeutic power of the imagination". He wrote, "the cunning man's greatest asset was his client's imagination; and in view of what is known today about the potentialities of any cure in which both doctor and patient have complete faith, its power cannot be disregarded". The patient who has faith in his doctor, the sufferer who is convinced that his proposed treatment will work, the afflicted person who accepts the path to recovery prescribed by his religion, his guru, his God or gods, is contributing a vital element to his wholeness of being. This is as important, for example, in Buddhist belief as in Christian or Jewish: hope is an essential ingredient of any medicine. This suggests in turn that healing is an art as well as having some basis in science, and that therefore the ritual surrounding it must engage the whole personality. In tribal cultures it may well be that there is a degree of psychological release and reassurance not so easily found in western medicine. Thus, Africans "may cherish the dramatic side of magical healing, the ritual acting-out of sickness, and the symbolic treatment of sickness in its social context. Primitive psychotherapy, in particular, can compare favourably with its modern rivals".

Here too Hippocrates, in a European setting, can entitle his essay *Decorum*, being advice to the physician as to his proper bearing and manner. He prescribes the doctor's style of "sitting, reserve, arrangement of dress, decisive utterance, brevity of speech, composure ... calm self-control" and advises that he should "give necessary orders with cheerfulness and serenity ... sometimes reprove sharply and emphatically, and sometimes comfort with solicitude and attention". In another culture the healer's authority may be expressed very differently. For example, a shaman may first dance himself (or herself) into a hypnotic trance, then lay hands on the afflicted person, tremble, moan or shriek, at which point the spiritual forces causing the sickness are understood by all to have been expelled and sent back to wherever they belong. Or the diviner will certainly wear impressive apparatus: horns[54] around his neck, amulets decorating his head, arms and legs, variously coloured beads and feathers, with powders, roots, and bones on

---

[54] Some healers in Malawi have attempted to give themselves Biblical legitimacy by citing the "horn of salvation" in Luke 2.69. This is rather a figurative expression emphasising the salvific efficacy of the Davidic Messiah. "Horn" in the Old Testament is a symbol of power, not part of the diviner's toolkit.

the ground around him. What is common ground between these disparate examples is the impressive display of *gravitas*, making evident the exercise of divinely given powers and so raising the patient's hope in expectation of his cure. It must be added, of course, that infection and disease, and certainly most gynaecological problems, need more of the doctor's science than of his art, although persuading patients to follow a curative regime in his absence belongs almost entirely to the latter.

The Hebrew response to sickness and suffering is set within its own ritual framework. The details are spelt out with great precision, especially in Leviticus 1-7 (dealing with the cult), but also chapters 11-15 (about being ritually clean or unclean), together with chapter 16 (on atonement). These sacred instructions, along with others scattered elsewhere in the Pentateuch, prescribe how all the various sacrifices[55] are to be performed. Even if they are not directly concerned with overcoming the consequences of sin, they still contribute to the maintenance of right relationships between God and his people, and so uphold their well-being. They also specify what must be done if, in various ways, pollution or disharmony have struck; implicitly, therefore, relating misfortune to an offence before God rather than as the effect of demonic influence. Thus the rites have both a restorative and a preventative function: the contagion of impurity is removed and the ever-threatening dangers of disorder are averted. Illness or the ill-effects of disturbing the social order may still be apparent, but sacrificial rites, together with the regulations about purity, are a means of containing the damage. Essentially the benefit of sacrifices, and any other ritual requirements, is peace of mind for both the individual person and the community of God's people, enabling them to stand with confidence before God.

The circumstances in which one type of offering was more appropriate than another are not made entirely clear in the Hebrew Bible, nor is it very evident what channels of guidance were available to the people (given that in other cultures it is usually the *diviner* who makes the connection between sin and sacrifice, linking the individual's private anxieties to the public cult). Broadly speaking, what was offered depended upon the status of the one who had sinned (compare Lev 4.3,13,22,27) as also upon the person offended (e.g. a ram for sacrilege against God, but a ewe for harming a neighbour). Even early rabbinic commentators found exegetical problems, perhaps because the rites underwent several stages of development in the course of Israel's history,

---

[55] One may compare the main sacrifices among the Basotho of Southern Africa today: *kananelo*, at childbirth; *sesila*, cleansing from sin; *poelanyo*, for reconciliation; *pha-badimo*, thanksgiving for ancestors.

as did the priesthood itself. For example, it may be that the holocaust (or whole burnt offering) and the "peace" (or well-being) offering were joined later by the sin and guilt offerings, perhaps after the construction of the Jerusalem Temple. Texts in the historical and prophetic writings also witness to a variety of usage, which makes it difficult to be over-specific about any particular offering. Sin offerings may have replaced the holocaust in time, and the "priestly school" (P) may have particularly encouraged cereal offerings[56], at least to supplement the animal offerings, an emphasis that may have helped to differentiate the Israelite religion from its rivals.

The "burnt offering" of Leviticus 1.3 is intended to effect "atonement" (v4 cf 9.7; 14.20; 16.24)) for the worshipper, who identifies himself with the animal by laying his hand on its head, with God. Here he appears to kill the animal himself, but in Ezekiel 44.11 it is described as the task of Levites. Passages in 1 and 2 Samuel describe occasions when the holocaust was offered (by Samuel and Saul in the face of the Philistines, by David to avert plague) in order to appease God's wrath. The "well-being" offering is outlined in Leviticus 3.1-17, and again in the priestly instructions of 7.11-36. Here the animal is shared between God, the priest and the worshipper, together with his household. It might be offered in thanksgiving, as part of a vow, or as a freewill sacrifice (7.14-15), although once again these are not clearly distinguished. In all such sacrifices there are references to the odour "pleasing to the Lord" i.e. to the re-establishment of a right relationship with God, at the same time restoring the social fabric within the community of Israel.

Particular interest attaches to the sin offering and the guilt offering. Both appear to concern one who sins unwittingly (4.1; 5.15), and it is hard to distinguish them, unless in Numbers 28 and 29 (concerning the major feasts of the year) it is the more public nature of the sin offering that stands out. The sin offering is prescribed in 12.6 as necessary for a woman after childbirth, although here it is the flow of blood, rather than an actual offence, which has rendered her unclean: on this occasion what is required is more of a purification rite. Again, the epithet "unwittingly" can hardly apply in 5.1, where a person has refrained from giving evidence of facts known to him at a public hearing. As for the guilt offering mentioned in 5.14ff, where a person fails to render his religious dues, he is certainly required by way of restitution to add one-fifth to its value; and perhaps, being a sacred matter, he feels unduly conscience-stricken about it - hence the description as a "guilt"

---

[56] These feature prominently in Leviticus; compare Genesis 1.29, which omits any reference to animal meat as food.

offering. The emphasis throughout these verses[57] is not upon the morally wilful nor upon deliberate reprobates but upon those who, without realising, infringe the divine ordering of society, thereby provoking the possibility of retribution. Yet 6.1-7 requires the guilt offering to be made also where deliberate fraud, deception, injustice, indeed sin "in any of all the things which men do", has been perpetrated. Once again, full restitution plus one-fifth of what was taken must be made. The apparent contradiction with Numbers 15.30-31, where anyone who sins "with a high hand" must be cut off from the people, is probably explained by a specific reference here to God's judgment on those who "murmured" in the wilderness. They would certainly fall dead (Num 14.32-33) and would not enter the promised land with the rest of God's people. As for the death penalty prescribed for blasphemers (Lev 24.12) and sabbath-breakers (Num 15.34), the texts seem to suggest the advisability of a further word from the Lord before its final enactment.

How far those texts which "cut off" the deliberate sinner were heeded in practice must be uncertain. The law of circumcision (Gen 17.14) could presumably be monitored more closely than either the consumption of leavened bread during the Passover festival (Ex 12.15) or any infringement of the sexual taboos listed in Leviticus 18.6ff. Judgment is certainly pronounced on prominent offenders such as the blasphemous sons of Eli (1 Sam 3.14); but while we are reminded in 1 Samuel 15.29 that God is not a man "that he should repent" (i.e. change his mind), elsewhere the ancient affirmation of Exodus 34.6-7 rather emphasises God's mercy, "forgiving iniquity and transgression and sin". It appears from Leviticus 16 that the annual Day of Atonement, *Yom Kippur*, kept as a solemn festival on the 10th day of the 7th month Tishri, provided a means of cleansing, first for the High Priest himself (v6), then of "the holy place" (v16), the tent of meeting (v17) and the altar (v18), but finally - with the aid of a live goat, symbolically driven into the wilderness - for "all the iniquities of the people of Israel, and all their transgressions, all their sins" (v21). The people were personally required to "afflict" themselves (vv29,31), and tradition took this to mean abstention from food and intercourse. The fast is referred to in Zechariah 7.5, an indication that from the time of the exile onwards the day assumed greater importance. Every 50th year a trumpet was to be sounded on this day (Lev 25.9-10) to announce a year of Jubilee, which was intended as an amnesty on debt and slavery, together with the restoration of ancestral property.

---

[57] Compare Numbers 15.22-26, dealing with the congregation's hidden faults, as well as vv27-29, concerned with the individual's.

There is, however, no evidence that any Jubilee was actually kept in post-exilic times, and it seems likely that it was put forward by the priestly school as a more realistic (because less frequent) alternative to the earlier sabbatical (7 yearly) remissions of Deuteronomy 15, which were seen to have been poorly observed. Equally, the provision of a scapegoat on the Day of Atonement has been claimed as an additional, indeed highly visual, remedy to prevent an accumulation of unremitted sin such as led inexorably to God's visitation of exile upon his people. The cleansing rites that preceded it can be understood as the necessary purification of the Temple and its altar at the start of each new year; but the ritual of the scapegoat is a tacit admission that the sacrificial system as practised thus far could not be wholly relied upon. "Azazel" (Lev 16.8) is shrouded in obscurity. Some commentators interpret it as a rocky cliff over which the goat was driven (usually by a non-Jew) to its death, while others, perhaps more plausibly in view of later usage in 1 Enoch and elsewhere, saw it as the name of a demon. At a profounder level the choice of the scapegoat by lot may have been a reminder of God's earlier election of his people: the historic coupling of names – Isaac and Ishmael, Jacob and Esau, indeed Judah and Israel – illustrates the truth that election is never by merit. Mary Douglas goes further in observing[58] that "the converse is also true" i.e. demerit does not wholly explain misfortune, even though it may be a contributory factor. This insight would thus anticipate the book of Job.

A striking feature of all these regulations is the emphasis placed upon the moral and cultic purity, not just of the priestly caste, as might be required in other ancient near east cultures, but of the whole population at large. Israel is set apart to be a holy people (Lev 19.2; 20.26; 22.32 cf Ex 19.6, taken up in 1 Pet 2.5), and must know that their health and prosperity depend upon keeping God's laws, whether of an apparently ethical or of a ritual nature. Another way of expressing this requirement is to say that they must remain within the boundaries prescribed by God for them. To cross a forbidden boundary was always dangerous, indeed life-threatening. The ultimate danger was to make contact with the divine, as in Exodus 33.20 where Moses is told, "You cannot see my face, for man shall not see me and live". God and man needed to be kept apart, as did clean and unclean people. Impurity resulted whenever the divinely given ordering of things broke down, an order expressed with greatest clarity in the priestly school's account of creation (Gen 1.1-2.3). To mix two things together was taboo: "You shall not let your cattle breed with a different kind; you shall not sow your field with two kinds of seed; nor shall

---

[58] Mary Douglas: *Leviticus as Literature (Oxford, 1999)*

there come upon you a garment of cloth made of two kinds of stuff" (Lev 19.19); or again, "You shall not plough with an ox and an ass together" (Deut 22.10). The detailed regulations about child birth, menstruation, ejaculation, disease, and dealing with corpses, result from the necessity to prevent whatever must be kept apart from making contact, and for providing remedies where impurity has occurred.

The treatment of a leper clearly indicates this rationale. It has little to do with more modern ideas of isolating those with contagious diseases. First, Leviticus 13.9-11 specifies that a man whose skin is partially white and partially raw flesh (i.e. giving a "mixed" appearance) is to be pronounced unclean. When he is totally covered by the leprosy (v13) he is considered clean, but as soon as any raw flesh reappears he reverts to being unclean again (vv14ff). Those who were unclean had to live apart (vv45-46), wearing the signs of mourning or loss (cf Ezek 24.17), so that others would not be contaminated with impurity (whether or not they caught leprosy themselves). Further, should a leper recover altogether, a guilt offering to make atonement had to follow (14.18,21). Atonement of a similar nature was also needed for the cleansing of a house (14.48-53), both rituals including a "scapebird" (14.7,53). The Priestly code probably increased the degree of social and religious exclusion imposed upon the chronically ill beyond what obtained in pre-exilic times, a tendency exemplified also in the Qumran community much later on. Early Christianity, by contrast, can be seen as challenging "the priestly health-care system".

In her classic work *Purity and Danger* (*London, 1966)* Douglas proposed an interpretation of some features of Israelite society, which has largely stood the test of time, viz. identifying religious and social boundaries with political ones. Thus, forbidden animals stood for the surrounding nations, clean animals were the Israelites, and sacrificial animals were the priests. The inability to eat unclean animals in fact prevented Israelites from mixing with those who did, so served a practical as well as a symbolic function. The sanctuary was also fenced against pollution, with the prohibition that any priests who were blind or lame, injured or with any kind of blemish, could not approach the altar. Even today, when there is no longer a Temple, observant Jews have not altogether abandoned the idea of ritual purity and the implied world-view behind it: that is to say, wholeness and health, together with preservation from disorder, are seen as dependent upon keeping faith with a God of order, who has made distinctions of many kinds for man's benefit.

Yet such a world-view, although forged more coherently by priestly thinkers in the embers of Judah's defeat by Babylon, cannot necessarily stand up any better when tested by reality. Rigorous performance of ritual and liturgical requirements was inadequate to prevent disasters befalling the nation, and even additional precautions (such as the scapegoat of *Yom Kippur*?) could offer no guarantee. Time and again there had been the prophets' warnings, not invalidated by the passage of years, of the people's misplaced hopes. There could be no peace of mind for the wicked, a constant theme of their pleadings and threats over several centuries. Indeed, there are some passages apparently repudiating the sacrificial system as a whole. "I hate, I despise your feasts ... Even though you offer me your burnt offerings and cereal offerings, I will not accept them" (Am 5.21-24). Again there is Isaiah, "Bring me no more vain offerings ... Your new moons and your appointed feasts my soul hates" (Isa 1.13-14), followed by Jeremiah, "Your burnt offerings are not acceptable, nor your sacrifices pleasing to me" (Jer 6.20) and also "Do not trust in these deceptive words: This is the temple of the Lord, the temple of the Lord, the temple of the Lord" (7.4). The psalmist adds his mocking voice, "Do I eat the flesh of bulls, or drink the blood of goats?" (50.13), and agrees with the prophets, "The sacrifice acceptable to God is a broken spirit" (51.17) - although the concluding verse 19 here looks to the day when once again right sacrifices will be made, leaving unresolved the debate whether it is the ritual that is deficient, or the worshippers themselves. Deuteronomy 12.11, by allowing only God's "name" to be present in the Temple, suggests a certain distancing from the ritual. The Deuteronomic school is sympathetic to the view that sin is expiated as much by prayer and good deeds as by sacrifice.

In post-exilic times, Isaiah 58.3-7 is in more radical vein: "Is such the fast that I choose, a day for a man to humble himself? ... Is not this the fast that I choose: to loose the bonds of wickedness, to undo the thongs of the yoke?" Centuries further on, after the rededication of the Temple, even ben Sira, who certainly appreciated its ceremonies (describing in 50.1-21 the splendid appearance of Simon, son of Onias, as High Priest), still found it necessary to issue words of caution. "A sacrifice from ill-gotten gains is tainted ... the Most High has no pleasure in the offerings of the godless, nor do countless sacrifices win his forgiveness" (34.18-19), which to the scrupulous at least must have sounded as a counsel of despair: for who can stand blameless before God?

The Shadow of Death

No healer, however skilled, could finally hope to cheat death; no sacrifices could buy an endless succession of years; no diviner could even promise uninterrupted prosperity, let alone immortality. "We must all die, we are like water spilt on the ground, which cannot be gathered up again" (2 Sam 14.14). In the earlier days of Israel's history, it was accepted that a dead person went to sleep with his or her ancestors (e.g. Solomon with his "fathers" in 1 Kings 11.43), and that the land of departed spirits, known as Sheol or the Pit, was below ground (e.g. Gen 37.35; Num 16.30 - a particularly graphic account of Korah's household being swallowed alive). Its gates are sometimes mentioned (e.g. Isa 38.10; Ps 9.13; 107.18), as in Egyptian or Mesopotamian accounts. Of funerary offerings there is very little evidence, apart from a possible reference in Deuteronomy 26.14, but it seems the dead were considered not wholly cut off from the living. The very fact that necromancy was condemned so fiercely is indicative of a popular belief that, while the departed were necessarily enfeebled, it was still possible, even if illegitimate, to communicate with them. The shades, according to Isaiah 14.10, could be aroused to speak to new arrivals: "You too have become as weak as we! You have become like us!" If their sleep could be disturbed by the living, that is, by mediums, or by the newly departed, it must also be true that they were not beyond God's reach. "Though they dig into Sheol, from there shall my hand take them" (Am 9.2): a verse paralleled by Isaiah 7.10-11, "Ask a sign of the Lord your God; let it be as deep as Sheol, or high as heaven". Psalm 139.8 also witnesses to God's cosmic presence, "If I make my bed in Sheol, thou art there!" But there is also a warning therefore that death can never be a complete escape from retribution: "a fire is kindled by my anger, and it burns to the depths of Sheol" (Deut 32.22).

In time, however, and understandably during the long years of exile, the possibility of any contact with the dead, good or bad, seems to have drained away. Sheol had now become a place lacking any semblance of life. It was all darkness and gloom, as in Psalm 88.6, "thou hast put me in the depths of the Pit, in the regions dark and deep". Once in Sheol, also now known as Abaddon ("the place of destruction" v11 cf Proverbs 15.11; 27.20; Job 26.6; 28.22), there is no escape (v8). The dead ("the shades" of v10) have no strength (v4), lying forsaken and forgotten even by God (v5). "The dead do not praise the Lord, nor do any that go down into silence" (Ps 115.17). In Sheol all things, even worship itself, have ceased: "death cannot praise thee" (Isa 38.18). It is a place of sheer hopelessness: "in death there is no remembrance of thee" (Ps 65.5). The only consolation was that the memory of the righteous would survive their passing "for ever" (Ps 112.6), while by contrast any remembrance of evildoers would be "cut off" from the earth (Ps

34.16).

The book of Job is full of this pessimism about death: "As the cloud fades and vanishes, so he who goes down to Sheol does not come up" (7.9); "I shall lie in the earth; thou [*God*] wilt seek me, but I shall not be" (7.21); "As waters fail from a lake, and a river wastes away and dries up, so man lies down and rises not again; till the heavens are no more he will not awake, or be roused out of his sleep" (14.11-12). In 10.22 the abode of the dead is a "land of gloom and chaos, where light is as darkness"; if the Pit can be called one's father, it is the worm who is one's mother or sister, reducing everything to dust (17.14,16). Yet such is Job's conviction about the injustice of his fate, he can even believe the impossible: that after his total disintegration (19.26) he will ultimately be vindicated. It is not clear whether this in any way presages a hope in his own exceptional revival, or whether it is solely his unshakeable faith in God's justice one day pronouncing a verdict in his favour. Both thoughts have, however, the seeds of future development within them.

Qoheleth also asserts the finality of death. "There is no work or thought or knowledge or wisdom in Sheol" (Eccl 9.10). All things come to an end, he reflects in 12.1-8: "the silver cord is snapped ... the golden bowl is broken ... the pitcher is broken at the fountain ... the wheel is broken at the cistern" - so too "the dust returns to the earth as it was, and the spirit [*the breath of life*] returns to God who gave it" (v7). "The fate of the sons of men and the fate of the beasts is the same; as one dies, so dies the other. They have all the same breath, and man has no advantage over the beasts; for all is vanity. All go to one place" (3.19-20). The rhetorical question of v21 concerning any difference between man, whose spirit is thought by some to go upwards, and the beasts whose spirits go downwards, is dismissive in its tone. It indicates there might have been some contemporary discussion of man's destiny, or alternative views known to Qoheleth in neighbouring cultures. But for him this is foolish speculation, admitting of no possible resolution within the very limited horizons of man's thought. There is one question that is settled: communication with the dead, or their return to earth in any shape or form, is unthinkable.

However, contact with a wider world of thought in Hellenistic times, and reflection on Israel's own bitter experience, does seem in due course to have borne fruit, allowing earlier intimations of an afterlife eventually to have reached fuller expression. Among these intimations there were those singular characters within Israel's history whom God preserved from death's decay. Enoch is mentioned in Genesis 5.24: he "walked with God; and he was not, for God took him" (cf Heb 11.5), which gave rise to much later Jewish speculation in the books of Enoch. The same passage also records remarkable longevity in those who, unlike Enoch, did eventually die. This characteristic is also found in the ancient Mesopotamian list of kings, implying that in ancient days the human race was an altogether hardier breed. But there follows (Gen 6.3) God's determination to limit the human lifespan to one hundred and twenty years, although this is not realised in Noah (9.29) nor in his descendants as far as Abraham's father Terah (11.10-26). The patriarchs also easily exceeded this limit, indicating that they were men of great stature before God (25.7; 35.28; 47.28). At a later date Moses, however, was (exactly) "a hundred and twenty years old when he died; his eye was not dim, nor his natural force abated" (Deut 34.7). The inference to be drawn is that his life was checked deliberately by God. The mention in v6 that his burial place was unknown "to this day" fostered later speculation that he had actually been taken by God himself. Finally there is the unambiguous account (2 Kings 2.10-11) of Elijah's own bodily assumption into heaven.

For many centuries, just as the word "death" could be used figuratively of any diminution of life, so too the imagery of resurrection was but a metaphor, signifying either recovery from deep distress or sickness (Ps 17.15; 73.24) or a revival in the nation's fortunes (Hos 6.2; Ezek 37.12; and arguably in Isa 26.16-19, although the LXX version differs). The idea of a dying and rising god was no doubt familiar from Canaanite mythology (e.g. Baal), but it had no place in Israel's faith. When therefore in Hosea 13.1 the prophet notes that Ephraim who has indulged in Baal worship has suffered death, there is a touch of irony. The accounts of miraculous restoration to life in 1 and 2 Kings performed at the hands of Elijah and Elisha do not offer any new insights into human mortality; but the incident in 2 Kings 13.21, where the bones of the dead Elisha retained wonder-working power, foreshadows the Christian Church's veneration of saints and martyrs and the associated cult of relics. It can be argued that a few passages (Jer 15.19-21; Ps16.8-11; 49.15; 73.25-26 - all cited in the early Church as pointing to the risen Christ) show some dawning recognition of the worth of the individual to God, alongside that of his chosen people Israel, and hence begin to challenge the tradition that one's future is limited to being remembered for one's deeds and within one's family. However, ben Sira at quite a late date thought it sufficient that "their line will endure for all time ... and their name lives for ever" (Sir 44.13-14).

It was not until the Maccabaean struggle of the 2nd century BC that acute questions of divine justice began to call for radically new answers, albeit drawing upon the principles seen at work in the preservation of Enoch and

Elijah, meditated upon in Isaiah 52-53, and wrestled with in Job: namely, that God, who punishes sinners with death, must surely have a reward other than final, and sometimes sudden, extinction for those who have heroically upheld his cause. Hence, "many of those who sleep in the dust of the earth shall awake, some to everlasting life, and some to shame and everlasting contempt" (Dan 12.2 - the only text in the Old Testament where there is unequivocal belief in life beyond death). Those to be rewarded in this way include the wise (v3) and "those who turn many to righteousness" i.e. the outstanding leaders of God's people. 2 Maccabees, written somewhat later as a spirited defence of Judaism (the first use of this term) against Hellenism, includes memorable defiance of Antiochus Epiphanes in chapter 7. "Fiend though you are, you are setting us free from this present life, and the King of the universe will raise us up to a life everlastingly made new, since it is for his laws that we are dying" (v9). Other brothers being martyred utter similar words (vv11, 14, 36), relying upon "God's promise to raise us again" (cf Heb 11.35). Atoning sacrifice for these heroes is mentioned in 12.43-45, being described as "a fit and proper act" (v43) taking "due account of the resurrection" which must be their "splendid reward" (v45).

It is somewhat ironic therefore that another work, the Wisdom of Solomon, from approximately the same period has found its place alongside 2 Maccabees in the Apocrypha. The idea of the dead being awoken from sleep (as in Dan 12.2) does not occur in Wisdom, which reflects the growing influence of Platonic and Stoic philosophy. It speaks movingly in 3.1-9 of the immortal reward of the virtuous. "The souls of the just are in God's hand ... though in the sight of men they may suffer punishment, they have a sure hope of immortality ... God has tested them and found them worthy to be his". There is some conceptual distance between the expectation here and that of the brother who in 2 Maccabees 7.10 displayed his hands and his tongue as members that, if amputated by his torturers, would be restored to him after death. Indeed, in Wisdom 8.19 there appears to be a belief, not only in the *athanasia* (immortality) of the soul, as contrasted with the *anastasia* (resurrection) of the body, but in its pre-existence as well. A taxing question about "untimely death" is considered and answered in 4.7ff: one who died young in God's service did not languish for ever in a state of immaturity, but "in a short time came to the perfection of a full span of years".

These and related ideas on the possibility of a future life were taken up in other inter-testamental and apocalyptic writings, entering the mainstream of Judaistic thought. Josephus in *Antiquities 18.1* mentions that both Pharisees and Essenes held that souls could survive death, although there were others such as the Sadducees who retained the old beliefs about the finality of death. 2 Esdras (4 Ezra), dating from after the fall of Jerusalem in 70 AD, preserved a little surprisingly in Christian rather than in Jewish circles, has a detailed account of the soul's fate after death. Apart from a privileged few of the saints who gain immediate access to heaven "without ever tasting death" (6.26), others have a brief foretaste of what lies in store, but then await the Last Judgment, when all are raised from the dead and final separation of the righteous and the wicked takes place. The righteous are described as waiting in an abode of "undisturbed peace" (7.85), which is also the "storehouse of souls" supervised by the archangel Jeremiel (4.35-36), but the wicked must "wander in torment, endless grief and sorrow" (7.80). It should be noted though, that the departed, pending God's verdict on their lives, were not thought to be accessible any more to the living, in the way that many Africans would hope their ancestors, at least the so-called "living dead", would continue to guide and bless them. Nor would prayer for the departed, feared to have fallen short in their lives, have any effect in winning God's favour (7.102-105, in contrast to 2 Macc 12, as above). However, God was known down the years to be compassionate, and to be forgiving towards any who repented. "Without his continued forgiveness there could be no hope of life for the world and its inhabitants" (7.137); yet in the end "only a few will be saved" (8.1-3).

It is of significance that in 2 Esdras, as in later writings of the Hebrew Bible (Zech 1-6; Dan 8-9,12), an angel is responding to, if not always answering, Ezra's questions. For by now it is angels who are considered, again with the exception of the Sadducees (Acts 23.8), to be the foremost spiritual interpreters and intermediaries.

Spiritual Powers at Work

That God is one, and that he is a sovereign Lord, are not immediately self-evident propositions[59], however familiar they may now appear to adherents of the main semitic faiths, Judaism, Christianity and Islam. Just as there are

---

[59] Herodotus, the Greek historian who lived during the 5th century BC remarked from his wide experience, "All men have their own ideas about the divine, and they all consider theirs to be the best". One may note too the sage comment in a recent writing of Rabbi Jonathan Magonet, "If our problem is the struggle to find a suitable image of God for our times, the problem of the Biblical period is the superabundance of gods. The designations and names ... never cease to flow from the pages of the Bible."

myriads of people coexisting or contending within the physical and material realm, so it might be supposed that something similar happens at a spiritual level in the unseen and intangible world. Interaction between what is seen and what is unseen is also a matter where many and varying interpretations can be posited, and need scrutiny. Within the history of Israel there is clearly some development in such ideas, with terminology and its application subject to change over the years. However, as is generally the case, officially sanctioned or written expressions of faith cannot always be assumed to represent popular understanding and usage. No doubt alien or superstitious elements lingered on, while possibly new and even incompatible elements were imported through contact with neighbouring cultures. Here personal names in the Bible, which often include some element of a deity's name, are a useful clue, while archeological remains such as seals and amulets, together with inscriptions on pottery, provide a broader background for interpretation.

"Your fathers lived of old beyond the Euphrates ... and they served other gods" (Josh 24.2). Given the emergence of the Hebrew people within the broad context of the Fertile Crescent, it is hardly surprising that many reminiscences of Mesopotamian or Canaanite "nature" religions are to be found in the Old Testament; in particular, not infrequent reference to the high god El, later identified with Yahweh. Alternation of the names Elohim and Yahweh is found in the Pentateuch, with the Yahwist (J) claiming the latter name was of ancient usage (Gen 4.26 cf Gen 14.22, an apparent attempt to connect Yahweh with "God Most High", worshipped of old in Salem) while the Priestly school (P) associated him specifically with Moses (Ex 6.2-3 – and perhaps with the faith of his Kenite father-in-law Jethro?). The rabbinic interpretation was that these two principal names represented different aspects of God, Elohim referring to the attribute of justice and Yahweh to that of mercy.

In Israel's earlier traditions there is evidence (suggesting henotheism rather than strict monotheism[60] at this time) of some plurality among the recognised heavenly beings; for example, localised deities, the gods of other tribes or

---

[60] Israel was perhaps not first in the field here: monotheism was officially decreed in 14th century BC Egypt during the reign of Akhenaton, the "heretic pharaoh", but abandoned after his death. For him Aten the sun-god was supreme, but he seems to have counted himself and his consort as close seconds. Margaret Barker in her book *The Great Angel: a study of Israel's second God (London, 1992)* argues that, while it was chiefly the Deuteronomist School which attempted to impose monotheism on Israel, many traces remain of older beliefs which in fact influenced much later teaching and practice.

nations, along with Yahweh's own assistants. At one point Jephthah warned the king of the Ammonites to keep to his own territory: "Will you not possess what Chemosh your god gives you to possess?" (Judg 11.24) Or again, in the mid 1970s two inscribed jars dating back approximately to 800 BC were found in the Negev, with painted inscriptions to "Yahweh of Samaria", "Yahweh of Teman" and "Yahweh and his Asherah", the last-mentioned suggesting an association with a sacred tree or pole. Although Israelites saw themselves as "the people of Yahweh" (Judg 5.13), who had no rival "among the gods" (Ex 15.11), it was still possible for Solomon to build shrines opposite the Jerusalem Temple for foreign gods such as Ashtoreth, Chemosh and Milcom (1 Kings 11.7; 2 Kings 23.13-14). There were apparently also in Yahweh's Temple figures of two cherubim (1 Kings 6.23-29 cf Ex 25.18-22; Ps 80.1), mythical creatures who guarded Eden (Gen 3.23 cf Ezek 28.14). The Decalogue (Ex 20.3) insisted that Yahweh alone should be worshipped, and (v4) forbade any divine images. However, in a number of texts (including perhaps Gen 1.26 and 3.22) Yahweh is depicted as presiding over a heavenly council. Psalm 82 in particular describes how other gods, with their respective responsibilities, presumably for the affairs of other nations (vv2-4), are accountable to him (cf Ps 138.1). They are "sons of the Most High" (v6)[61], but God "holds judgment" in their midst (v1) and can determine their fate (v7). He is in fact ruler of the whole earth (v8). "All the host of heaven" is mentioned in 1 Kings 22.19-23. There are reckoned to be "ten thousands of holy ones" (Deut 33.2), who are also "the sons of God" described as shouting for joy along with "the morning stars" at the dawn of creation (Job 38.7). But there is a warning against astral worship[62] in Deuteronomy 4.19, and the king of Babylon, with "astral" ambitions, can be depicted (Isa 14.12) as a fallen Day Star. All the sons of God (Ps 29.1-2) are called upon to worship God, who is "great and terrible above all that are round about him" (Ps 89.6). It seems to be suggested in Deuteronomy 32.8-9, at least in the LXX version, that to each of these other divine beings was allotted charge over a particular people, who "spread abroad on the earth after the flood" (Gen 10.32); while (v9) "the Lord's portion is his people, Jacob his allotted heritage". Ben Sira, writing much later, is straightforward on this point: "For every nation he appointed a ruler [*i.e. a heavenly being*], but Israel is the Lord's portion" (Sir 17.17). Heavenly administration of this sort became of course conceptually

---

[61] Quoted by Jesus in John 10.35 when defending his own claim to be "Son" of the Father.

[62] This accusation is later made in Stephen's speech before the High Priest (Acts 7.42-43).

viable with Israel's experience of imperial rule.

It is plain from the prophecies and warnings of Hosea that religious infidelity continued in his day (8th century BC) among the people of Israel. They frequently offered sacrifices to the Baalim, and lacked the "knowledge of God" (Hos 4.1). For Amos it is clear that God's sovereignty extended over all the neighbouring countries as well, for he is the one "who forms the mountains, and creates the wind, and declares to man what is his thought" (Am 4.13). There is a verse later (9.7), "Are you not like the Ethiopians to me, O people of Israel?", which challenges the very notion of any subordinate, or "national", deities. In turn, Isaiah ascribed the fall of Samaria and the deportation of much of the rural population to Assyria to God's judgment on their pagan cults: "you shall be ashamed of the oaks in which you delighted" (1.29). In the following century the Deuteronomic school prescribed death as the punishment for any form of apostasy (Deut 13.6-11), while Josiah mounted his reforms under what has been described as a banner of "self-conscious monotheism". Jeremiah soon afterwards could scathingly dismiss other gods as "broken cisterns, that can hold no water" (Jer 2.13), which is the implied position of Zephaniah as he looked to the day when all nations would bow down to Yahweh (Zeph 2.10-11). Psalm 97.7 describes the worthlessness of idols, but still allows that there may be other gods who themselves "bow down" before Yahweh. Most explicit is the assertion of Deutero- Isaiah (45.5): "I am the Lord, and there is no other, besides me there is no God".

While the Priestly writers also promoted this teaching, the Pentateuch still retains a number of heavenly beings, who are not necessarily of divine status, although it is debatable how far the terminology (of "angels", for example) is a linguistic device to avoid mention of the divine name. It is of interest to note the views of the early Church fathers. "Economic" theologians such as Justin and Tertullian were prepared to see, in the words of Irenaeus, "the Son of God scattered everywhere in the scriptures"; whereas Augustine insisted in *De Trinitate* that whatever was seen, heard or apprehended in these visitations might represent, but could not be, divine being itself. In that perspective "the sons of God" mentioned above (and in Gen 6.2, reappearing also in Job 1.6; 2.1) would be reckoned as of angelic rank. There is a theophany in Genesis 18, when Abraham saw the appearance of three "angels" in their normal guise of men. In v22, one is identified with Yahweh himself, who remains to talk with Abraham, while the other two angelic beings continue towards Sodom. Likewise in the account of Isaac's sacrifice, it is initially God who speaks to Abraham (22.1), but later an angel (vv11,15) calls him twice, speaking God's words. Jacob's wrestling at Peniel (Gen 32.22-32) is with an unnamed man, also described as an angel in the version of Hosea 12.4-5; he is discovered (v28) to be God himself - a story not dissimilar from the strange episode of Exodus 4.24, where the Lord met Moses "and sought to kill him". The functional identity of "the angel of the Lord" with Yahweh is found in the call of Moses, in his experience of the burning bush (Ex 3.2 ff), as in other "angelic" encounters (Judg 6.11ff; 13.15-22). In these instances there may have been editorial modification to accommodate heightened sensitivity to God's transcendence. The identity seems less clear when the angel of the Lord appears in military guise (Num 22.23; 2 Sam 24.16-17; 2 Kings 19.35), described in Joshua 6.13 as "commander of the army of the Lord". Jacob himself encounters a host of them, whom he describes as "God's army" in Genesis 32.1. Of course, the Hebrew word *malak,* used for angel, may on occasion simply mean a human messenger (as in Gen 32.3), sometimes leaving the interpretation slightly uncertain (as on Elijah's journey in 1 Kings 19.4ff).

In post-exilic times the emphasis on God's otherness from men led to an increasing hierarchy within the ranks of heaven, and more frequent angelic mediation. There was, for example, a growing tradition which attributed the promulgation of the Law of Moses to angels: an angel "spoke to him at Mount Sinai" (Acts 7.38 cf v53; Gal 3.19; Heb 2.2). There is too a differentiation of role: for example, of the two angels named in the Hebrew Bible, Gabriel (Dan 8.16; 9.21) reveals God's future plans while Michael (Dan 10.13,21; 12.1), described as one of the chief princes, defends the cause of Israel against the other princes, who feature rather like the gods of the nations mentioned earlier. Raphael, another of the seven archangels, is named in the book of Tobit and is generally associated with a ministry of healing, while Uriel occurs in 2 Esdras, and in 1 Enoch to regulate the movement of the stars. It is hardly surprising that confusion arose over their activities: Hermas, an early Christian writer, seems to have identified Michael with Jesus, as perhaps the Qumran community did with Melchizedek. The Talmud suggests that the names of the angels were imported when the Jews returned from captivity in Babylon; they certainly feature in Zoroastrianism, the old Iranian religion later adopted by the Persian rulers.

At a time when the military might of foreign powers was being bitterly experienced, its heavenly counterpart was that of rebellious angels. Isaiah 24.21-23 recognises the existence of evil, even in high places, and envisages God's complete ascendancy being achieved only on "the day of the Lord" when (v21) the hosts of heaven will be punished. Job is another later writing which ascribes to angels the freedom to make moral choices. "His angels he charges with error" (Job 4.18), so they too are judged (21.22) and brought into line (25.2). Ultimately, though, it was envisaged that God's kingdom would prevail and the holy ones (the angels / the sons of God) would worship him in heaven alongside all his faithful people (Dan 7.27).

The emergence of Satan as God's principal angelic enemy was a late development of Second Temple Judaism. Martin Buber noted[63], "The early stage of Israelite religion knows no Satan: if a power attacks a man and threatens him it is proper to recognize Yahweh in it or behind it, no matter how nocturnally cruel or dread it may be." It is not surprising that the strongly monotheistic Amos can ascribe all things, good and bad, to God's own agency. "Does evil befall a city unless the Lord has done it?" (Am 3.6)[64]. The expression of his righteous judgment often demands this, and Psalm 78.49 suggests that "destroying angels" may be the instruments of his wrath. Or, of course, as in Jeremiah 4.6, God may use the might of a foreign army: "I bring evil from the north, and great destruction". His omnipotence is summed up in Isaiah 45.7: "I form light and create darkness, I make weal and create woe, I am the Lord who do all these things". Yet other passages suggest that his supremacy is not achieved without some struggle. There is in Genesis 1 a darkness "upon the face of the deep" (v2), which needed subjugation by God's Spirit. Order had to emerge out of a formlessness which might have been chaotic, and only then is God's creation pronounced as good. In the account of Genesis 2.4ff, alongside the many blessings of Eden is found also "the tree of the knowledge of good and evil" (2.9), while in 3.1 appears the beguiling serpent (whose identification as the devil seems to occur for the first time in Wisdom 2.24). Mythic imagery continues in several Psalms e.g. "Thou didst break the heads of the dragons on the waters. Thou didst crush the heads of Leviathan" (74.13-14 cf 104.26), and again, "Thou didst crush Rahab like a carcass" (89.10 cf Job 9.13; 26.12). But such were the sufferings of God's people, the fight can be seen as not yet finally concluded: "In that day the Lord with his hard and great and strong sword will punish Leviathan the fleeing serpent, Leviathan the twisting serpent, and he will slay the dragon that is in the sea" (Isa 27.1).

Such graphic descriptions of the forces of wickedness need not seduce us, however, into positing that opposition to God's ways is found anywhere other

---

[63] M.Buber: *Moses (Oxford, 1946)*
[64] The moral theologian Fr. Benezet Bujo has expressed the view in *Christmas, God becomes Man in Africa (Nairobi, 1995)* that "the general mentality of black Africa sees evil as coming from man, not from God".

than in human hearts and minds, or in the known enemies of God's rule (but see 4.1 below), any more than the personification of wisdom in the book of Proverbs need be taken as an inroad into strict monotheism. Prophetic hyperbole needs to be recognised for what it is, and not taken too literally. Jeremiah recognised the root of most human failing: "The heart is deceitful above all things, and desperately corrupt; who can understand it?" (Jer 17.9). Or, as Genesis 6.5 puts it, "The Lord saw that the wickedness of man was great in the earth, and that every imagination of the thoughts of his heart was only evil continually". Indeed, "the hearts of men are full of evil, and madness is in their hearts while they live" (Eccl 9.3). Hearts are often "stubborn" (Jer 18.12), "stony" (Ezekiel 11.19; 36.26), "hardened" (Ex 7.22 etc; Zech 7.12), or simply "proud" (Prov 21.4); and hence certainly needing spiritual renewal ("a new heart"), as emphasised particularly in exilic times first by Jeremiah (24.7) and then by Ezekiel (e.g. 18.31).

But God may sometimes test his people's hearts (as observed already in his encounters with Jacob, and then Moses). It is a complaint of the prophet (Isa 63.17) that God's seeming abandonment of Israel has caused a loss of faith and of righteous behaviour. In Genesis 22, by contrast, God seems to be asking too much of Abraham in the sacrifice of his son Isaac. The scene is similar in the book of Job, but now with a member of God's council being given permission to test Job's faith, and to see if suffering will turn him towards evil. This "accuser" or "adversary" is Satan, met in that role in Numbers 22.32, standing in Balaam's path. Or again, Hadad the Edomite is a "satan" challenging Solomon in 1 Kings 11.14. Whereas his role in Job is legitimate, he appears in his accusation against Joshua as High Priest (Zech 3.1-2) to have overstepped the mark: "The Lord rebuke you, O Satan!" In the rewriting by the Chronicler (1 Chr 21.1) of David's census (2 Sam 24), for the first time Satan, used now as a personal name, appears to act in defiance of God's wishes. Later writings give him other names, such as Mastemah (Jubilees 10.8), Semyaz (1 Enoch 6.3) and Belial (Zadokite Document 4.13)[65]. Sin and human mortality are explained in this literature as the result of a heavenly rebellion (1 Enoch 1-6; Jubilees 5.1-11), an extreme dualism not met within the Hebrew Bible, but somewhat mitigated in Jubilees 15.31: "Over all nations [*God*] has placed spirits in authority to lead them astray from him." We may note too that "the lying spirit" of 1 Kings 22.21-22 is but an angel in

---

[65] Some medieval scholars of demonology ascribed to a hierarchy of seven archdemons the seven deadly sins: Lucifer (pride); Mammon (avarice); Asmodeus (lechery); Satan (anger); Beelzebub (gluttony); Leviathan (envy); and Belphegor (sloth).

God's service acting an uncharacteristic part (and perhaps little more than a *dramatis persona* in Micaiah's tale), while the "evil spirit" from Yahweh that afflicted Saul (1 Sam 16.14-23; 18.10; 19.9) is chiefly descriptive of the depression and paranoia that settled upon him following God's rejection of him as king (1 Sam 15.26-28).

As noted already (3.1), a fear of demons also resurfaced in this intertestamental period, reflected, for example, in certain verses of the Psalter as translated into the Greek Septuagint. Thus Psalm 91.6 has in Hebrew the word "wastes", which the LXX - originating significantly from Egypt - reads as "a demon". These came to be seen as evil spirits subject to Satan himself, through whose agency he could deceive and torment people in works of continued hostility towards God. In Rabbinical literature individually named demons were considered to be responsible for specific sicknesses or ill-effects, and professional exorcists[66] came into prominence in 1st century AD Judaism. References can be found in e.g. The Testaments of the Twelve Patriarchs, as in the Genesis Apocryphon, both of which were known to the Qumran community; and in Josephus' Antiquities, where he even suggests that King Solomon practiced exorcism of old. Apocalyptic writers viewed the activity of demons as coterminous with "this evil age", and therefore any challenge to them as a sign that God's new age was beginning to dawn.

---

[66] Note Matthew 12.27 and Acts 19.13.

Chapter 4

Christian Affirmations

Deliverance from Evil

When writing to the Romans, Paul mentioned the whole array of forces in the universe that might beset the Christian believer: as cited earlier (1.1), "neither death, nor life, nor angels, nor principalities, nor things present, nor things to come, nor powers, nor height, nor depth, nor anything else in all creation, will be able to separate us from the love of God in Christ Jesus our Lord" (8.38-39). The significance of most of these entities within the Hebrew Bible has now been explored, and it is time to examine Paul's assertion of faith in closer detail. In what ways does the New Testament substantiate his claim? How does belief in the Lordship of Jesus Christ address the fears and uncertainties that have surfaced in the various Old Testament, and indeed Apocryphal, writings - most of which are kin to the anxieties, distresses and problems of any age?

It is clear that in 1st century AD Palestine, as elsewhere in the Graeco-Roman world, the activity of evil spirits was widely assumed. Within Judaism it came into greater prominence (above, 3.4) largely as a result of closer contact with other cultures, and so may be termed a "syncretistic" belief. Jesus himself did not challenge this belief, and, in so far as he exercised power over evil spirits, demonstrated that his ministry was of potentially universal significance, meeting the needs of Jews and Gentiles alike. To a later generation, imbued with a scientific cosmology, the reverse begins to seem more likely. Enlightened minds find it to Jesus' discredit that he did not reject the very notion of evil spirits, a refusal which limits his credibility and makes him a prisoner of his own day and age, a less - rather than more - universal Saviour.

There is in fact a divide within the modern Church on this issue. On one side are the Biblicists, who recognise Jesus as an exorcist, along with charismatic Christians, who exorcise demons themselves in the power of the Holy Spirit. On the other side are Christian psychiatrists, more inclined to interpret mental disorder within an entirely different framework of reference, and theologians who claim scientific rationality as one of God's precious gifts (cf ben Sira on the skills of a physician, 3.1 above). But there is more to be said in this debate. In the first place, Jesus' ministry of exorcism is not as extensive as his ministry of healing, and is actually rather different from that of a diocesan or latter-day exorcist in that Jesus does not appear to spend any time diagnosing the causes of disorder[67], but responds directly to requests made to him. In Mark 1.24 the initiative rests with the unclean spirit (a spirit that makes a person "unclean"). This person's entry into the synagogue already suggests something amiss there. The possessed in Mark 5.2 is found in a more likely place viz. among the tombs and even has a more likely name, "Legion", derived from the unclean Romans. It is no surprise to find here in Mark 1.32 that Jesus' many healings take place (symbolically as well as actually) outside the synagogue when the Sabbath is over. This demon recognises and names Jesus, in an attempt to gain control of him, but Jesus first necessarily silences and then expels him. Above all, the emphasis is upon Jesus' authority (vv22,27), a theme taken up in Mark 3.20-30 where the accusation is made that Jesus is in league with Beelzebul, once the name of the god of Ekron[68], but now applied to Satan who is "the prince of demons". Recognition of Jesus' authority occurs also in Mark 5.7, and in 7.24ff and 9.14ff appeal is again made to him to take action. Mark 3.27 interprets such action as the "binding" of Satan (which proved impossible in 5.4 until Jesus' arrival on the scene). This features in much apocalyptic eschatology, ushering in God's kingdom (Mt 12.28; Lk 11.20). Respective verses a little later in these two gospels (Mt 24.43-44; Lk 12.39-40) indicate that Satan as much as anyone else is ignorant of God's plans, and is taken by surprise whenever "the Son of man" comes. One passing incident in Mark 9.38-40 may suggest that exorcism was viewed differently across the church communities. If the disciple John, who "forbids" it in v38 (but is overruled here by Jesus, as in Lk 9.49), is connected with the "Johannine community", which seems to claim a higher Christology and so is cautious about others who use the name of Jesus, it might help to explain the absence of exorcisms in the fourth gospel.

In the second place, there is the story in Luke 13.10-17 of a woman with crippling curvature. She had "a spirit of infirmity" (v11), and Jesus accepts that in some way this is the work of Satan (v16), the one who "binds" others. There is no mention, however, of the woman's sins, and significantly for this discussion it is not an exorcism that is performed. Jesus does not cast out an evil spirit, but simply lays hands upon the woman. It is therefore open to us to

---

[67] For example, the German catholic bishops' conference ruled in 1998 that medical and psychiatric treatment should be tried before resorting to exorcism.
[68] 2 Kings 1.2: note also the names Belial in 2 Corinthians 6.15, a passage that agrees with the Essenes in seeing him as the leader of darkness, and Apollyon in Revelation 9.11.

say that the mention of Satan here is equivalent to saying that the woman's condition was objectively evil i.e. contrary to God's will and purpose. Or put another way, the phrase "spirit of infirmity" is a figure of speech used a little differently from the term "unclean spirit". Further, Luke 10.20 suggests that Jesus himself did not encourage too strong an emphasis upon his disciples' powers of exorcism: "do not rejoice in this, that the spirits are subject to you; but rejoice that your names are written in heaven". In fact, they need to be aware (v18) that their local triumphs are simply signs of a cosmic struggle going on in heaven itself, so it is the engagement between Jesus and Satan ("the devil") himself to which our attention is directed once again (cf Lk 4.1-13[69]; 22.39-46). The saying found in Matthew 12.43-45 (Lk 11.24-26), in which "seven other spirits more evil" (cf Lev 26.21) return with the one expelled to make "the last state of that man" worse than the first, also indicates that exorcism on its own is little enough: we may recall here that there were Jewish exorcists, particularly belonging to the Pharisees' party. A response of faith to God's gracious deliverance is also needed, such as that of the women "healed of evil spirits" who stayed with Jesus (Lk 8.2-3). Or one can say that the coming of God's kingdom is not only marked by the defeat of evil, but there are also positive indications that his rule is visibly being implemented (Lk 4.18-19 cf 7.18-23). Certainly this is the view expressed in Matthew 7.22-23, where even successful exorcism in the Lord's name is no compensation for not doing God's will.

Thirdly, when one looks beyond the synoptic gospels, where the disciples are indeed commissioned "to cast out demons" (Mk 3.15; Mt 10.1,8; Lk 9.1), there is little mention of exorcism elsewhere in the New Testament. Luke makes general references in Acts (5.16; 8.7) and recounts specific events at Philippi (16.16-18) and Ephesus (19.11-17) where Paul himself is the exorcist who enables "the name of the Lord Jesus" to be "extolled" (19.17). It should be recognised though that Luke sees the Church's ministry (as recorded in Acts), reflecting that of Jesus (as recorded in his gospel). Other examples include, the outpouring of the Holy Spirit, healing miracles, Stephen's martyrdom and final words, the apostles' and then Peter's dramatic release from prison (equivalent to Jesus' tomb), Philip's scriptural exegesis and sudden disappearance (like that of Jesus at Emmaus). But the gift of "exorcism" is not referred to by Paul in his own listings of spiritual gifts, unless it is covered by the word "miracles" (1 Cor 12.10; 2 Cor 12.12; Gal

---

[69] In Matthew 4.1-11 the text reveals Christ's obedience in contrast to Israel's disobedience in the wilderness, while the briefer report in Mark 1.13 hints at a coming restoration of paradise.

3.5). Nor is it found in the catholic epistles, the Johannine letters or Revelation, despite the strong awareness of "the devil" and his ceaseless activities (e.g. 1 Pet 5.8). James comments (1.14), "each person is tempted when he is lured and enticed by his own desire", and notes the "passions that are at war in your members" (4.1) without even hinting at the presence of evil spirits. Again, John selects his "signs" with care, but none of these are exorcisms. In fact, the issue in the fourth gospel is as in Mark 1.27 and the Beelzebul controversy, namely the source of Jesus' authority. In John 7.20; 8.48ff; 10.20-21 the accusation is made that he acts and speaks as he does because he himself is possessed by a demon: in reality his life and death mean the overthrow of "the ruler of this world" (12.31; 14.30; 16.11 cf Mt 4.8-9; Lk 4.5-6, where the devil lays claim to "the kingdoms of the world"). So it is once again Jesus' own conflict with "the evil one" (17.15) to which attention is drawn. The disciples will continue to have "tribulation" (16.33); but they can be of good cheer, as Jesus has "overcome the world". Pilate shortly after these words comes on the scene in the guise of an earthly ruler, boasting of his power (19.10), but he is reminded he has no power except that allowed him by God (v11). This insistence counter-acts any incipient dualism in this gospel, as does the quotation of Isaiah 6.10 earlier (12.40 cf Mt 13.14; Acts 28.26-27).

As to the reality of demons or evil spirits, the Christian need not be over-dogmatic, noting that neither the Apostles' nor the Nicene Creed address this issue. As observed previously (see 3.4), it is not inconceivable that within God's creation there is a hierarchy of beings. Indeed, such would seem to be implied in the Priestly perspective of Genesis 1, with emerging forms of life differing in complexity, both as regards physical / biological structure, and with respect to the capacity for self-determination, mental consciousness, and spiritual awareness. Today the possibility of other rational beings elsewhere in the universe is a commonplace of scientific talk, as is the existence of other universes. Within this context the existence of spiritual beings different from ourselves can surely be more easily accommodated than formerly, without the straitjacket of Newtonian physics. Logic would further suggest that if there are angels (whom rabbinic tradition would claim as sharing with human beings the fourfold abilities of speech, sight, understanding and upright posture), there can also be fallen angels, those who turn against God's will (in 1 Jn 3.8 from the very "beginning"). Further, such sin would not be a sin of the flesh but of the spirit, which is represented in the Bible as the more dangerous. Paul, for example, warns his readers in Ephesians 6 of "the wiles of the devil" as also of "the spiritual hosts of wickedness in the heavenly places", with, be it noted, little concern for whether "the evil one" is singular or plural. There are apparently for Paul "world rulers" and "powers", occupying a much lower heavenly place than Christ, as noted in 1.21, but it is not clear how far these are just metaphors for any forces opposed to God, summed up in "the prince of the power of the air" of 2.2. He does, however, suggest in 1 Corinthians 6.3 "that we are to judge angels"[70]. Again, Paul's condemnation in 1 Corinthians 10.20-21 of any participation in pagan feasts is directed against divided loyalties and a weakening of Christian faith: on the one hand the "demons" (or demi-gods), like the idols that represent them, are for Paul non-existent (9.4-6), but on the other hand he knows how dangerous it is to allow any openings for unprincipled syncretistic attitudes. There is considerable wisdom in his warning, "let anyone who thinks that he stands take heed lest he fall" (10.12).

In today's world it is possible that for some, as John MacQuarrie has expressed it[71], "The evils once attributed to demons - sickness of body or mind, failure of crops, infertility of herds, and so on - are now understood in different ways. The once extensive empire of the demons has shrunk away". But he adds rightly that we should not take too superficial a view of evil and its "superhuman dimensions". Hans Kung likewise warns[72] against trivialising the power of evil, which is "substantially more than the sum of the wickednesses of individuals", but cannot be located wholly in any demonic entities - for then (e.g.) Hitler and Stalin could be portrayed as mere "victims" of Satan. The use of the word "sin" in the New Testament points in the same direction. In the Synoptic gospels it often occurs in the plural, indicating people's particular transgressions; whereas in other places, in the singular (e.g. Jn 8.34, but notably in Rom 5-7, as in the Dead Sea Scrolls), it is an evil force exercising power over people, "enslaving" them. In Freudian terms, mention must be made too of the libido, "a seething, boiling cauldron of desire that seeks to erupt from beneath the threshold of consciousness". Demons, from this point of view, could then be redefined as projections of the unregulated drives of a person that lead him or her to act regardless of any effects upon others.

Leslie Newbigin once made the interesting suggestion that among the principalities and powers that rule western society today are the many

---

[70] Compare the Twelve's role judging the tribes of Israel in Matthew 19.28 (Lk 22.30).
[71] John MacQuarrie: *Principles of Christian Theology (London, 1977)*
[72] Hans Kung: *Credo (London, 1993)*

mindsets and ideologies: "isms"[73] such as materialism, racism, sexism and individualism, together with prevailing "attitudes" of corruption, cynicism, or perhaps apathy. Even the obsession with political correctness is verging (cf 1.6) on becoming demonic in character. It may be that these are also modern equivalents of the "philosophy and empty deceit" mentioned in Colossians 2.8, which are "according to the elemental spirits of the universe" (a somewhat obscure phrase). Nevertheless, in other cultures, for example in Africa, as in past Christian centuries in Europe, the dominant powers and spirits may be conceived or named differently. In so far as any of these is considered to have an objective, personalised existence, it remains an epistemological question of some difficulty to know how one such spirit or demon could genuinely be differentiated from another, given that its mode of presentation might actually be manifold. There must, therefore, be a degree of arbitrariness in classifying such spirits which, no doubt, is why Paul can switch readily from singular usage ("the devil") to the plural ("spiritual hosts of wickedness"). By contrast, there is a sure ground for Trinitarian discourse in the very human form of Christ's own person, and in the revelation received through him. Biblical language about the power or powers of evil is on the other hand legitimately variable, and arguably desirable from a pastoral point of view, in line with Paul's wisdom to be (as appropriate) "all things to all men" (1 Cor 9.22).

There is no doubt, however, that, whatever particular framework of thought is preferred, evil is portrayed in the Bible as a dangerous and still threatening reality that, apart from Christ, can in many different ways overwhelm both individuals and the whole of society. For example, Satan "immediately comes and takes away" the word of the gospel (Mk 4.15), and "the tempter" can quickly destroy faith already implanted (1 Thess 3.5). But here is the central gospel message: that in Christ evil has met its match - its ultimate defeat - and that therefore those who have faith in Christ will not finally be separated from him.

This is expressed in various ways. The most powerful statement is in Hebrews 2.14-15: "that through death he [*Christ*] might destroy him who has the power of death, that is, the devil, and deliver all those who through fear of death were subject to lifelong bondage". Paul writes of Christ, that on the Cross he "disarmed the principalities and powers" (Col 2.15), as he also "abolished in his flesh the law of commandments and ordinances" (Eph 2.15)

---

[73] Thomas Hardy in his novel *The Woodlanders (London, 1887)* links Dr. Fitzpiers' acquisition of "books on some mysterious black art" to his being "too deeply steeped in some false kind of 'ism".

- a point emphasised too in Romans 8.3 and 2 Corinthians 5.21 where Paul is thinking of sin as a power holding human beings captive. In 1 Corinthians 15.42ff his focus is on death as the enemy; he uses the analogy of a (perishable) seed buried in the ground, but bursting later into new (imperishable) life, an idea developed in Romans 6.

John 12.24 has similar imagery: "unless a grain of wheat falls into the earth and dies, it remains alone; but if it dies, it bears much fruit". The Cross is then described in almost Archimedean[74] terms: "Now shall the ruler of this world be cast out; and I, when I am lifted up from the earth, will draw all men to myself" (Jn 12.32). In Revelation 5.6ff this is envisioned in the Lamb standing before the throne "as though it had been slain", and being pronounced worthy to receive honour and might from all God's creatures (including myriads of angels) on account of having ransomed innumerable people for God. The victory is pictured in the symbolic tribute of Mark 15.39: "And when the centurion [*a man of the godless ruling nation*], who stood facing him, saw that he thus breathed his last, he said, Truly this man was the Son of God".

Arising from this, the call is confidently made in the New Testament again and again to resist "the devil" (Eph 4.27; Jas 4.7; 1 Pet 5.8-9), that is, "the evil one" who appears to have the world in his grip (1 Jn 5.19). For now, through the Holy Spirit gifted to his Church, the Christian has all the armour and protection he needs (Eph 6.13ff), not least truth (v14) in the face of evil's many deceits. In the Mortimer Report on Exorcism[75] attention is drawn to the main characteristics of evil. Recollecting that Christ is the Logos and indeed the wisdom of God, it follows that what "turns away from God becomes increasingly non-rational and so sub-rational ... Demonic forces lead to a confusion and degradation of personalities". Pope John Paul II once pointed out that "temptation is nothing else but directing towards evil everything which man can and ought to put to good use". But further, this can easily be disguised from us. "Satan disguises himself as an angel of light" (2 Cor 11.14), which means his agents also masquerade in deceitful ways. No doubt Judas, into whom Satan entered (Lk 22.3 cf Jn 13.2), was convinced he was doing God's work. The devil, according to John 8.44, "is a liar and the father of lies" (and so the father of liars, deceivers and all manner of falsity e.g. Ananias in Acts 5.3). The devil and Satan is "the deceiver of the whole world" (Rev 12.9). He was even "that ancient serpent" of cosmic origins (Rev 20.2), and hence long-practised in his ways. John the Seer can also call

---

[74] "Give me a place to stand, and I will move the earth."
[75] *Report to the Bishop of Exeter on Exorcism (London, 1972)*

Satan by his name "accuser" in Revelation 12.10, but this is a parody of his former role in that he is lying to God about the faithful. However, the earlier idea (found in Job 1-2) does seem to be present in 2 Corinthians 12.7, where Paul is given "a thorn in the flesh" as "a messenger of Satan" to keep him from being too elated.

"Now the Spirit expressly says that in later times some will depart from the faith by giving heed to deceitful spirits and doctrines of demons" (1 Tim 4.1). The Christian paradox is that, as God's time approaches nearer, so opposition to him intensifies. Nowhere is this portrayed more vividly than in Revelation, where, although the devil's final fate, which is to be thrown into the symbolic "lake of fire and sulphur" (20.10), is certain, nevertheless his activity will increase so as to test God's people to the limit. "Behold, the devil is about to throw some of you into prison, that you may be tested, and for ten days you will have tribulation. Be faithful unto death" (2.10). Indeed, an hour of trial is coming on the whole world (3.10), what 1 Peter 4.12 describes as "a fiery ordeal". It is of course through his agents that the devil operates. These are described as angelic in Revelation 12.7 (cf Mt 25.41), but also include kings, armies and merchants, especially of Rome, false teachers and slanderers[76]. Perceptively, John the Seer also shows Satan's house as divided (cf Mk 3.23-26), leading to the self-destructive end of evil: "The beast will hate the harlot" (Rev 17.16).

Testing and tribulation certainly seems a perennial feature of Christian life, even apart from its eschatological dimension (as outlined by Jesus, for example, in Mark 13). It is of course the central paradox of the Cross, which is "a stumbling block to Jews and folly to Gentiles" (1 Cor 1.23): how can Christians preach victory with the ever-present reality of death, and how can we commend a gospel that speaks of suffering, that is, self-denial and a daily carrying of one's cross (Mk 8.34-35)? Who in fact will believe our report (cf Isa 53.1) so long as it speaks of "losing one's life"? On the walk to Emmaus (Lk 24.13-35), Jesus addressed this very issue. The hopes of Cleopas and his companion had been utterly confounded (v21) by the events of Good Friday. It seemed after all that the forces of darkness had imposed themselves yet again. The response from Jesus was twofold, in a way that came to be modelled by the Church in its eucharistic worship: a ministry of word (setting hearts on fire v32) and of sacrament (disclosing Christ's own presence v31, impelling mission v35). He first unfolded[77] the inner meaning of the

---

[76] It is no accident that the locusts of Revelation 9.7 have "human faces".

[77] Luke has already demonstrated that Jesus is the authority on scripture in his encounter with the devil (4.1-13), as in his prophetic exegesis at Nazareth (4.16-22).

scriptures (vv25-27), the significance of which for the present discussion being that the wicked acts of violence perpetrated against himself were by no means beyond God's control, and were actually allowed by him in fulfilment of his deeper purposes. Bearing in mind the correspondences between Luke and Acts, it can be suggested with some confidence that the servant songs of Deutero-Isaiah, pointing to Jesus' vicarious suffering, were central to the exposition, given the reading of such verses (specifically Isa 53.7-8) in the eunuch's encounter with Philip (Acts 8.26-40): the reference to entering "into his glory" (Lk 24.26) does, however, suggest the use of a variant text. Secondly, he revealed himself as alive and undefeated by the forces ranged against him, in a way that accorded with the life he had shared with his disciples previously (particularly in the breaking of bread as in Lk 9.16; 22.19). His identity and mission were therefore neither changed nor overcome by death. Indeed his presence had the power to call his disciples once again into his fellowship and service (as in Acts 2.42).

It is in that perspective and within that fellowship that Christians engage patiently and with long-suffering (and both these words or their cognates are in frequent use in the New Testament) in the struggle against evil. Our daily prayer, as taught by Jesus himself, is "deliver us from evil" (Mt 6.13). "We pray this in the conviction that God is a faithful and dependable protector who will give his help readily to all who ask and beg for it. Consequently, when we have prayed these words, there is nothing left to ask for."[78] Whether the evil lies within ourselves, or within others, or is of seemingly superhuman power, we know it is no match for the love of God revealed in Jesus Christ. Within God's purview it is possible for there to be a hopeful Christian evaluation of whatever faces us in life or in death. Luke indeed exemplifies this as he charts the early fortunes of the Church in Acts, illustrating how external setbacks such as arrest, imprisonment, persecution, trial and death were all discovered (e.g. as in 8.4; 28.30-31) to be new opportunities for serving and witnessing to God. It was left to later generations of Christians to reflect more fully upon the superabundance of grace in purging the inner man. Three examples may suffice: St. John of the Cross (1542-1591) in *The Ascent of Mount Carmel* described how even apparently positive images and aspirations may need to be dissolved by God, leading to the "dark night of the spirit", in which one's seeming abandonment is actually the decisive time of Christian transformation, and death is the moment of greater union with God's purpose. Again, Dante's great poem *The Divine Comedy* set in the year 1300 had earlier attempted a visionary journey, starting with the writer "astray in a

---

[78] Cyprian of Carthage: *On the Lord's Prayer*.

dark wood, where the straight path is lost". As it unfolds, he is harrowed and reduced to penitence by encountering ever deeper pits of human vileness, healed and educated by climbing the mountain of purgatory, and finally ascends through the circles of heaven, where he moves beyond words to a glimpsed vision of the Trinity itself, "the love that moves the sun and the other stars". If also, in the later gospels of Luke and John, St. Mary herself is the archetypical disciple, then symbolically the subsequent doctrines of her immaculate conception and her assumption witness to both the power and the triumph of divine grace in all believers.

The Promise of Abundance

The Easter message is not just about deliverance from the forces of evil. It opens up vistas of life beyond what has been experienced so far on this earth, what the fourth gospel calls "abundant life" (Jn 10.10). In fact the transfiguration of Christ (Mt 17.1-8; Mk 9.2-8; Lk 9.28-36) can be seen as a brief disclosure, not only of his own coming resurrection, but of the new life promised to God's faithful people. "Beloved, we are God's children now; it does not yet appear what we shall be, but we know that when he appears we shall be like him, for we shall see him as he is" (1 Jn 3.2). Again, 2 Peter 1.11 proclaims that "there will be richly provided for you an entrance into the eternal kingdom of our Lord and Saviour Jesus Christ". When the kingdom of God was preached by Jesus, he announced that it was "at hand" (Mk 1.15) or even "in the midst" (Lk 17.21). Prayer for its coming was also needed (Mt 6.10), if only, as Cyprian of Carthage commented[79], that Christians should thereby nurture their desire for it, as against the beckoning "glitter and power" of earthly kingdoms. Later in Mark, Jesus' imagery describes the kingdom as a seed growing mysteriously into a sheltering shrub (4.30-32), or maturing towards a rich harvest (4.8; 4.26-29). Entering "the kingdom of God" (9.47) is synonymous with entering "life" (9.43,45), which is actually "eternal life" (10.30), and may be likened to having "treasure in heaven" (10.21).

Paul speaks of "our glorification" (1 Cor 2.7), "what no eye has seen, nor ear heard, nor the heart of man conceived, what God has prepared for those who love him" (v9). And where John 17.3 identifies the essence of eternal life as knowing "the only true God, and Jesus Christ" sent by him, Paul refers similarly (1 Cor 13.12) to understanding fully, "even as I have been fully understood". It is that "face to face" meeting that eluded even the greatest of

---

[79] In the same meditation Cyprian urges "constant prayer and petition" lest Christians should fall away from God's (heavenly) kingdom.

Old Testament figures, a goal recognised too in Hebrews 12.14, where holiness is described as the virtue "without which no one will see God". Jesus himself, in his beatitudes, promises the vision of God[80] to "the pure in heart" (Mt 5.8); and at the climax of Revelation (22.4) God's servants will at last "see his face" in the new Jerusalem. Such language is necessarily metaphorical, and 1 Timothy 6.16 is therefore right to introduce a reminder of God's abiding transcendence even at the *epiphaneia* of Christ: God "alone has immortality and dwells in unapproachable light, whom no man has ever seen or can see". Where 2 Timothy 1.10 describes Christ as having brought *aphtharsia*, the Greek actually means "incorruptibility" i.e. imperishability rather than immortality. This is also the sense of 2 Peter 1.4 where believers are granted to become "partakers of the divine nature", a Greek idiom which by now had been adopted by some Jewish thinkers as well, without implying full divinisation. Augustine, in *City of God XXII*, comments, "God will be seen by the eyes of the heart which can see realities that are immaterial". For him, "God himself will be the goal of our desires; we shall contemplate him without end, love him without surfeit, praise him without weariness." Indeed, Gregory of Nyssa reflecting *On the Beatitudes* can affirm, "Whoever sees God has obtained everything of which he can conceive."

The full reality of salvation is still of course awaited, but its day has already begun to dawn. The casting out of demons is a sign that "the kingdom of God has come upon you" (Mt 12.28; Lk 11.20), and so are the different forms of healing. These are listed in Luke 7.22: "the blind receive their sight, the lame walk, lepers are cleansed, and the deaf hear, the dead are raised up, the poor have good news preached to them". And there are indeed instances of resurrection occurring at Jesus' hands. Jairus' daughter is brought back to life (Mk 5.35-43), as is the widow's son at Nain (Lk 7.11-17), and Lazarus at Bethany (Jn 11.38-44). In each case the evangelist insists that faith is a needful accompaniment. In Mark the scoffing crowd is put outside, while the child's father is exhorted, "Do not fear, only believe" (v36). In Luke the scepticism is encountered later in Jesus' comment of v32ff, that the men of this generation respond neither to John the Baptist's ascetic call to repentance, nor to Jesus' message of joy and forgiveness. We seem here to anticipate that later verse (16.31), "If they do not hear Moses and the prophets, neither will they be convinced if someone should rise from the dead", a remark concluding the parable of the rich man and Lazarus, but equally applicable to Jesus' rising from the dead. As for the fourth gospel, John explicitly relates resurrection to Jesus' own person: he is - in a series of "I am" statements -

---

[80] "Their angels", comments Jesus (Mt 18.10), "always behold the face of God."

"the resurrection and the life" (v25), and thus can say to Martha, "Did I not tell you that if you would believe you would see the glory of God?" (v40). Matthew, however, does not record such a miracle, even though Jesus' charge to the Twelve in 10.8 includes raising the dead, and Jesus' report to John the Baptist in prison makes reference to this happening (11.5)[81]. It is not in fact, in this first gospel, until after the moment of crucifixion, when Jesus "yielded up his spirit" (27.50), that we read (v52) "the tombs also were opened, and many bodies of the saints who had fallen asleep were raised".

Taking the gospels together, certain issues present themselves. The power of Jesus to defy even the claims of death is displayed in the individual "resuscitations". These enable us to appreciate that our mortality is not in God's intention necessarily our final state. And yet it is clear that each of the three - Jairus' daughter, the widow's son and Lazarus - will at some subsequent time succumb to death again (if Lazarus is, as some argue, the Beloved Disciple, this is implied in Jn 21.23). Their revival is of limited duration, but each time our eyes have been opened to glimpse a little of God's infinite mercy and the possibilities that may yet be ours in the future, given faith, as well as to prepare us for Christ's triumphant rising from the dead, God's miracle *par excellence*. Matthew's initial reticence, by contrast, has some theological justification. If the cross is when the devil's hold upon the world is finally broken (or however evil is thought to be defeated), then that is when death's dominion is ended too, so that the saints woken from death at that climactic moment will not now return to their sleep. Matthew is careful, however, to state that although "woken" they did not emerge from their tombs until "after his [*Christ's*] resurrection" (27.53)[82]. This is in line with the unanimous witness of the New Testament that Christ is "first-born of the dead" (Rev 1.4 cf Col 1.18), "the first fruits of those who have fallen asleep" (1 Cor 15.20,23), and "the first-born among many brethren" (Rom 8.29), who are therefore an *ecclesia* gathered by him and so "enrolled in heaven" (Heb 12.23).

But to treat of eschatological hopes as already partially realised is to invite both exaggeration and misunderstanding. Thus, some of the Dominical

---

[81] This verse reflects Isaiah 61.1-3 where mourners receive "the oil of gladness" i.e. the joy of seeing their dead alive again. Matthew perhaps includes this in preference to the clause about "liberty to the captives" in view of John the Baptist's own incarceration.

[82] The appearance of these saints (Mt 27.53) may be seen as fulfilling Zechariah 14.5: "the Lord your God will come, and all the holy ones with him". But this text may also be reflected at Mt 24.31.

sayings in the fourth gospel, taken out of the possibly under-stated context of Christ's death, may have led the unwary into error. In the story of Lazarus, the words "whoever lives and believes in me shall never die" (Jn 11.26), coupled with the earlier verse "he who believes in the Son has eternal life" (Jn 3.36), may have contributed to doctrinal problems being experienced within the Johannine Community. 1 John is at pains to set these right, with particular emphasis upon the expiatory significance of Christ's death (1.7; 2.2; 3.3,7; 4.10; 5.6), which may have been seen by "false" teachers as irrelevant. Concerns also seem to surface in Pauline circles. In 1 Corinthians15 there is a lengthy discussion of issues surrounding the idea of resurrection, with an earlier hint (4.8) that some may have considered themselves to be already in a risen state: "Already you are filled! Already you have become rich! Without us you have become kings!" Certainly we learn from 2 Timothy 2.18 that, in another congregation, Hymenaeus and Philetus "have swerved from the truth by holding that the resurrection is past already" - a teaching that became common among Gnostics in the 2nd century. Again, certain verses in the Pauline tradition - but taken out of context, which (as in Rom 6) actually implies that the Christian is "raised" from sin - may have lent themselves to this interpretation: "you were also raised with him [*Christ*]" occurs in Colossians 2.12 (cf 3.1 and Eph 2.5-6). The broader (corrective) picture, which employs the future tense, is however presented in other verses such as Colossians 1.22-23,28; 3.4,6, 24 (together with passages in Ephesians) where a conditionality is emphasised ("provided that you continue in the faith") and a warning given, that each must become "mature in Christ". Future fulfilment is emphasised also in 1 Thess 4.14; Rom 6.5; Phil 3.10-12.

If Jesus' miracles reviving the dead may be seen as signs of the approaching *eschaton*, and a foretaste of the Christian's inheritance, so may his other miracles too. Indeed, the writer of the fourth gospel is deliberately selective in presenting his readers with what he terms "signs" (Jn 2.12; 4.54)[83]. At the very least Jesus' signs, or miracles, must be seen as distinct from any magical associations: they are events pregnant with meaning, that reflect God's direct and purposeful action[84]. For John, they certainly point to the mystery of Christ's own being (e.g. 6.35), a hint of the glory to be revealed when his "hour" (2.4 etc) fully arrives. Mark also emphasises this authority, as in the *pericopae* noted already where Jesus confronts the forces

---

[83] There is also mention of "many" other signs in John 3.2; 20.30-31.

[84] "Miracles are presented to our senses in order to stimulate our minds ... and so make us marvel at the God we do not see through his works which we do see" (Augustine, *On St. John's Gospel*).

of evil, but also in his scriptural allusions (e.g. to Israel's exodus from Egypt, suggested in the miracles of feeding and walking on water) that promise eschatological fulfilment. Further meaning is hidden within the very language used, both here in Mark and in the other synoptic gospels. Several healings are actually described in terms of "resurrection": "he took her by the hand and lifted her up" (1.31); "rise, take up your pallet and go home" (2.11); "little girl, I say to you, arise" (5.41); "[Jesus] lifted him up, and he arose" (9.27); "take heart, rise, he is calling you" (10.49-50, where his mantle is symbolically discarded too). In similar style we read that when Levi responded to Jesus' call, "he rose and followed him" (2.14). All these suggest that there is life in Christ "before death", but point to a continuation of life "after death" as well. Mark does however warn of possible deception: false Christs may "arise" (13.22), with their own "signs and wonders" which may lead the elect astray[85].

In the time of the Church therefore, miracles and healings are not unambiguous, and Christians should not unreservedly set store by them (cf Mt 7.21ff), although undoubtedly through the mystery of God's own working they may well occur. Luke mentions a number of such in Acts (3.7 etc), but his focus here is chiefly upon Peter and Paul (cf 2 Cor 12.12, where Paul himself refers to "the signs of a true apostle") in their crucial role of bearing witness to the risen Christ. This mission is seen by Luke as now supplanting the commission to preach the kingdom, as recorded in his Gospel. In other Christians, however, he records God's grace working miracles of a different, but perhaps less spectacular, kind e.g. the remarkable generosity noted in Acts 4.32-37. As for the glossolalia (Acts 2.1-11; possibly 8.17; 10.46; 19.6) it can be argued that the phenomenon is not seen by Luke as universally available to all Christians, so much as a divine warrant authenticating important stages in the life of the Church[86]. Certainly Paul has to teach the charismatics of the Corinthian church some discernment as to the more important gifts of the Holy Spirit, and it is the less dramatic exercise of love which he singles out above all others (1 Cor 12-13 cf 14.18-19).

The tension between what is "already here" and what is "yet to come" runs through the New Testament. Paul can therefore speak of the Spirit as a "guarantee" (2 Cor 1.22; 5.5 cf Eph 1.14) which sets God's seal upon us in readiness for the promised heavenly inheritance. In Revelation (7.3; 9.4;

---

[85] In Revelation 13.3-4 there is even a parody of the resurrection, possibly Nero *redivivus*, leading "the whole earth" to follow in wonder.

[86] Key stages in Acts include the birth of the Church, its mission outside Jerusalem, its separation from John the Baptist's movement (cf Jn 1.33).

14.1) the same idea of being "sealed" is found, but portrayed as God's protection of his chosen ones against harm. Matthew prefers to describe this in terms of Jesus' own presence with his followers: "I am with you always, to the close of the age" (28.20), indeed "in the midst of" his gathered people (18.20). In what may be called this "interim" time there is both opportunity and difficulty. So Paul can testify (2 Cor 4.8ff), "We are afflicted in every way, but not crushed ... always carrying in the body the death of Jesus, so that the life of Jesus may also be manifested in our bodies". This agrees with the selfless principle commended in Mark 8.34: "whoever loses his life for my [*Christ's*] sake and the gospel's will find it". This is no easy challenge, which is why it is "hard", if not "impossible", to enter God's kingdom (Mk 10.24,27), except with God's help (v27). Few people, according to Matthew 7.13-14, find the way "that leads to life". But it is a paradox often observed that those with the least of this world's riches are among those readiest to share, and those who have experienced suffering among those best able to offer comfort and support to others. Thus is discovered something of the joy of Christian living, the "way" that leads to God himself (Jn 14.6), according "to the measure of the stature of the fullness of Christ" (Eph 4.13).

Yearning for God's future to come in all its plenitude is expressed again and again (e.g. 2 Pet 3.13), but perhaps nowhere more profoundly than in Romans 8: "The creation waits with eager longing for the revealing of the sons of God ... and not only the creation, but we ourselves, who have the first fruits of the Spirit, groan inwardly as we wait for adoption as sons, the redemption of our bodies" (vv19,23). Here there is a broad conception of God's purposes, envisaging his cosmic rule along with his reign on earth, where a later tendency may have been to identify this kingdom, at least partially, with the institution of the church. Matthew's parable of the wheat and tares (13.24-30) receives an interpretation (13.36-43) which illustrates this tendency. It is spelt out even more clearly in Colossians 1.13-14, with its language of two spheres: "He has delivered us from the dominion of darkness and transferred us to the kingdom of his beloved Son, in whom we have redemption, the forgiveness of sins". Paul describes himself in Colossians as a minister of "the church" (1.25), where earlier he has been a servant or minister of "God" (2 Cor 6.4). And in Ephesians 3.21 the doxology emphatically ascribes glory to God "in the church", as the body of Christ is being "built up" (4.13). The fourth gospel exhibits a related shift, from kingdom to the concept of eternal life. In turn this then becomes a focus upon the person of Christ (in whom that life is found) and "the flock" of whom he is the shepherd (Jn 10.1-18; 18.1-9; 21.15-19). Evidently with the passage of time attention began to be given rather more to the realities of living with one's fellow Christians[87]. The imminence of the Lord's coming, with its global and indeed cosmic implications, seems to have somewhat receded from view.

The Risen Lord

However the Christian hope is expressed, it is certainly the unanimous witness of the New Testament that it rests wholly upon what God wrought in and through Christ at the first Eastertide. As Paul emphasised in 1 Corinthians 15.14, "if Christ has not been raised, then our preaching is in vain and your faith is in vain". That Christ died for our sins and was raised on the third day is the bedrock of Paul's message, as of the entire Christian tradition (1 Cor 15.3). He recalls the evidence for the resurrection in the following verses, concluding with his own testimony (vv8-9) which for Christians today is particularly compelling, given his previous antagonism to the faith. Some of this material is recorded in more detail elsewhere, in the Gospels[88] and in Acts, where the evangelists are ready to defend their beliefs against popular

---

[87] In the Johannine writings, there is an incipient dualism between the Church and the world, with Christian love finding its expression almost confined to the former.

[88] The absence of any actual resurrection appearances in Mark's Gospel, with its abrupt ending ("for they were afraid / awestruck"), in the oldest manuscripts is one of the major puzzles of the New Testament. The predictions of Jesus' resurrection (8.31; 9.31; 10.32-34) may actually be contrasted with references to the coming of the Son of Man which will emphatically be *seen* (9.1;14.26,29) by his disciples. Hence the issue may be related to that of the delayed *parousia*, and Mark's emphasis upon the need to understand that "gaining life" is inseparable from the readiness to lose it (8.34ff). In chapter 13 Jesus has warned of much upheaval before the Son of man is seen coming in glory (v26). This may involve arrest and persecution for Christ's followers. But at last angels (v27) will come to gather the faithful; is the "young man" of 16.5 an intimation that the end times have begun? Indeed, is the removal of the stone (16.4) a hint of the old order being dismantled (13.2 mentions temple stones being taken apart)? The women certainly flee (16.8); is this the beginning of the final flight spoken of in 13.14? They are to go to Galilee (16.7), which may be the mountain of refuge in 13.14 (cf Mt 28.16). These speculations carry some support from the fact that other details of chapter 13 (especially the hours specified in v35) are certainly taken up in Mark's passion narrative. His message would thus be one of encouragement to a struggling church that the end has begun, and that soon therefore *they themselves will see* the risen Christ coming in glory. Hence he would agree with that final beatitude of the fourth gospel, "Blessed are those who have not seen and yet believe".

criticism. Matthew 28.12-15 knows of corrupt reports among the Jews about how the tomb came to be emptied, while Luke 24.36ff and John 20.24-28 (along with the clasped feet of Mt 28.9) answer those sceptics who consider Jesus' appearances were mere hallucinations. More importantly for Paul, and for Peter's sermons in Acts, is that what happened was "according to the scriptures". That is to say, the raising of Christ from the dead coheres with God's purposes revealed in many different ways through the Hebrew Bible, whose true meaning is disclosed only now. In fact, it might be said that the scriptures can at last be truly understood "according to Christ", so it is far more than a few selected texts that point to him. To ask "according to which passages or texts?" therefore misses the point. Luke 24.27 embraces the totality of scripture, describing how "he [*Jesus*] interpreted to them in all the scriptures the things concerning himself". This gives Christ's resurrection the proper context within which it is to be viewed, in whose absence it would be an isolated and mystifying event, a baffling and inexplicable marvel rather than the defining mystery of Christian faith[89].

What, we must now ask, is the significance of Jesus' resurrection? What is its revelatory value? What does it tell us about God and his created order? What bearing does it have upon the destiny of Christian believers themselves, or indeed of any other human beings? The logic of Paul's argument is well worth closer examination. "If the dead are not raised, then Christ has not been raised" (1 Cor 15.16) is an assertion whose validity clearly depends upon Christ being "in the likeness of men" (Phil 2.7). The issue would seem to be, Is it possible for any mortal man to live again after first dying? To which Paul's reply is, Yes, we have the example of Christ, hence it is a possibility for other human beings as well. Of course, the supplementary question follows, For which individuals then will this be a reality - for all, or for the chosen few? In fact, might not Christ be uniquely privileged, the only one on whose behalf God exercises his almighty power? It is here that Paul's statement of belief (1 Cor 15.3ff) is certainly "of first importance"; in particular, the clause that "Christ died for our sins". This is of course a compact testimony to God's saving love for all his people. Its validity depends this time upon Christ being also "in the form of God" (Phil 2.6). The fourth gospel expresses it memorably, "God so loved the world that he gave his only Son, that whoever believes in him should not perish but have eternal life" (Jn 3.16).

---

[89] As Christian writings came to have an authority of their own, forming a "New" Testament, so the Jewish scriptures came to be seen more as preparatory for this fuller revelation. The Old and the New, in Tertullian's words, were *aliud, sed non alienum*.

Jesus' words in the Synoptic Gospels, although expressed in rabbinical fashion, are also relevant. He speaks of God as "the God of Abraham, and the God of Isaac, and the God of Jacob - he is not God of the dead, but of the living" (Mk 12.26-27; Mt 22.32; Lk 20.37-38 adds the words "for all live to him" in this interpretation of Ex 3.6). Along with Matthew 8.11 (Lk 13.28), this indicates the same truth from a different standpoint. God's intention in creating human beings was for them to participate in an eternal relationship with himself. Although on the human side this may be rejected, the cross is the demonstration that nothing will diminish God's love for his people. So for Christ to be raised by God asserts the power of God's love in the face of evil, and at the same time sets his seal of approval upon Jesus' life and death, "glorifying" (Acts 3.13) and "exalting" (Phil 2.9) him. He can thus be seen as "the pioneer and perfecter of our faith" (Heb 12.2), who has opened a "new and living way" (Heb 10.20) into God's presence.

The mystery of what happened to Jesus at Easter can never adequately be charted. Certain facts are plain: the tomb was empty (Mk 16.3), hence his physical body had in some way been transformed. He was also seen, as Paul describes in 1 Corinthians 15.5-8, on a number of occasions in the immediate aftermath, but also after the elapse of some considerable time[90]. Acts 1.22 insists that an essential condition of being an apostle - that is, one replacing Judas - is to have seen the risen Christ. Accounts of some of the appearances suggest that at times Christ's risen body had the characteristics of a "physical" body, such as tangibility (Lk 24.39; Jn 20.27). Yet within the same encounter it could lose these properties and become in some way "immaterial", so as to disappear in a moment (Lk 24.31 cf Jn 20.19). Description of such a body clearly lies beyond words, but St. Thomas Aquinas used the terms "impassibility", "subtlety" (freedom from material restraint), "agility", and "clarity" (whereby the appearance exhibits true spiritual beauty, as in Christ's transfiguration)[91]. In the *hesychast* tradition associated particularly with the holy mountain of Athos, the vision of light sometimes experienced by the monks during prayer was interpreted as the same glory that once radiated from Christ's transfigured body, a view defended particularly by St. Gregory Palamas (died 1359) in the century after Aquinas.

Luke goes on to record (24.51) the ascension of the risen Christ as a final leave-taking of the disciples (discounting here Paul's later experience, and

---

[90] Paul does not distinguish in kind between his experience of the risen Christ and that of earlier witnesses.

[91] Or as with the righteous who "shine like the sun in the kingdom of their Father" (Mt 13.43).

perhaps that of the "five hundred brethren" mentioned by him). He describes him as being "carried up into heaven" (cf Lk 9.51; also Acts 1.11, which unlike the gospel account mentions a specific interval of forty days). Matthew 28.16 also implies an interval between the day of resurrection and the disciples' final commissioning, as does John 20.26 and the Galilee narrative of John 21. By contrast, the words spoken on the cross in Luke 23.43 suggest that Jesus' hope was to be "in paradise" that same day, just as Lazarus in the parable of Luke 16.19ff is carried within a short time to "Abraham's bosom"[92]. The language of "exaltation" used in Philippians 2.9 and in the letter to the Hebrews (where only in 13.20 is there explicit mention of the resurrection) carries a similar convergence of meaning. And in the fourth gospel the phrase "lifted up" (Jn 3.14 cf 12.32) perhaps embraces both crucifixion and resurrection, while Jesus' empowering of his disciples with the Holy Spirit occurs on Easter evening (Jn 20.22), unlike the delayed occurrence in Acts 2.

Given these conceptual interactions, it would seem to be a mistake to give the difficult passage of 1 Peter 3.18ff ("he [*Jesus*] ... preached to the spirits in prison") any definite chronology. RSV's "preached" (v19) can be read as "proclaimed", meaning that Christ's victory on the cross, leading to the subjection (v22) of all spiritual powers (cf Jn 16.11; Rev 12.10-11), was made known even to the most rebellious among them. The implication would then be that those who hear this letter, despite being in straightened circumstances (v17), can be assured of God's ultimate triumph. Nor in 1 Peter 4.6 ("the gospel was preached even to the dead") is there any need to take Christ as the preacher. It can be seen as a reminder that those who received the gospel, but have since died, may yet "live in the spirit like God" (cf 1 Thess 4.14-16), for certainly Christ is "Lord both of the dead and of the living" (Rom 14.9: cf Phil 2.10, where Paul is writing more with rhetorical fervour than with theological rigour, indeed perhaps citing here an early Christian hymn). 1 Corinthians 15.29, however it is interpreted[93], is certainly further evidence that Christians were concerned about the fate of the dead, just as their forebears had been in 2 Maccabees 12.38-46 and their progeny would

---

[92] A feature of the afterlife found also in 4 Maccabees 13.17 - "figuratively" (Heb 11.19) as Abraham received back Isaac (Gen 22.12).

[93] For example, as remedying what some may have considered, as a result of the factional spirit mentioned in 1 Corinthians 3.10-17, an inadequate baptism. In the modern world there is a genealogical cult of ancestors; this relies heavily on the International Genealogical Index managed in Salt Lake City, Utah by the Mormon Church, who offer - without sales pressure! - "a baptism of the dead".

continue to be for centuries afterwards. St. John Chrysostom commented on this passage, "Let us not hesitate to help those who have died and to offer our prayers for them".

Alive in Christ

This is the point at which the fate of the dead in Christian understanding must be explored further. It has been noted earlier that Hebrew thought focused much more upon the fate of Israel as a people than upon the question of personal survival. A saintly few might be taken directly into heaven, and martyrs in God's cause were also worthy of special consideration. But in general the focus was upon "that day" when God would restore the fortunes of his people, either here on earth (which would be of little benefit to the departed) or - latterly in apocalyptic thinking - in a radically new order which would include the righteous who had died already. The tension between these two poles of thought is present in the New Testament as well. On the one hand, the individual is of inestimable worth to God. For example, "even the hairs of your head are all numbered" (Mt 10.30), while there may be noted in the parables of Luke 15 a strong emphasis upon the lost one who is sought or prayed for until found. In time, this emphasis came to undermine any narrowly ethnic dimension of salvation, and enabled Peter, followed by Paul, to declare: "Truly I perceive that God shows no partiality, but in every nation any one who fears him and does what is right is acceptable to him" (Acts 10.34-35). But on the other hand, as in the African tradition of *umunthu* ("I am a person because of other people"), there is a strong corporate identity to Christian existence, expressed by Jesus in the symbolic appointment of the Twelve and then, for example, by Paul in his image of the body. "We, though many, are one body in Christ, and individually members one of another" (Rom 12.5). The fourth gospel uses here the analogy of a vine and its branches (Jn 15.1ff), with further emphasis in the farewell discourse of Jesus upon mutual indwelling.

Stress on the value of the individual together with the importance of the community are both reflected in New Testament teaching about death. Both strands are present in Paul's thinking too. In what is probably his earliest extant letter, 1 Thessalonians, there is concern about Christian brothers and sisters who have already died (4.13), whom Paul describes as being "asleep". On the day of the Lord's coming, however, they will be the first to rise, and then all will meet the Lord "together" (v17). The Christian's final destiny is to be in a community that will "always be with the Lord" (v17). In

Philippians the issue of his own future presses upon Paul, who is now in prison. It would certainly help the understanding of Paul's theological development to be able to locate this imprisonment either in Ephesus, in the middle of the 50s, or else in Rome, at the end of that decade i.e. to know whether or not Philippians preceded his Corinthian correspondence. There is however no definitive evidence. While he hopes to be released (Phil 2.24), that cannot yet be certain. So Paul reflects upon the two possible outcomes: "to me, to live is Christ, and to die is gain" (1.21). When in 1.23 he speaks of "choosing", it is probably to be thought of as "preferring". "I am hard pressed between the two", he writes, "my desire is to depart and to be with Christ, for that is far better. But to remain in the flesh is more necessary on your account" (vv23-24). Here Paul conceives that if he dies he will have left behind "the flesh" and will at once be "with Christ" (as the penitent thief was promised in Lk 23.43 - a divine generosity which shames our human readiness to condemn). This surely indicates more than a state of "sleeping". In similar vein, 1 Peter 3.18 describes Jesus as "being put to death in the flesh but made alive in the spirit". Nevertheless, Paul in the same letter (Phil 3.20-21) reminds his readers that collectively their hope lies still ahead. Christ will come from heaven, which is where Christians have their true *politeuma* or "citizenship", so as "to change our lowly body to be like his glorious body". Beyond death, it would appear then quite unambiguously that Paul's hope is to be "with Christ", whereas full participation in the life of heaven must await further divine action.

1 Corinthians appears closer to the presentation in 1 Thessalonians. Those who have died are "asleep" (15.20), awaiting God's action at the coming of Christ, when "those who belong to Christ" will be raised (v23) as "spiritual" (God-related cf 2.13ff) rather than as "physical" beings (v44). Paul retains the word "body" here, which indicates the relational aspect of existence, but avoids the dualistic language of a soul or spirit "having" a body. In 5.5 a notoriously immoral man is excommunicated by Paul "for the destruction of the flesh, that his spirit (*pneuma*) may be saved in the day of the Lord Jesus". The interpretation of this verse is uncertain, although some "chastening" may be noted elsewhere in the Pauline corpus (1 Cor 11.32; 2 Cor 12.7; 1 Tim 1.20). Clearly, however, whatever the "spiritual body" may be like, it has ceased to be of a fleshly nature. The word soul (*psyche*) is used a number of times elsewhere in the New Testament, generally to be translated as the "self" (e.g. Mt 10.28; Heb 13.17; Jas 1.21; 1 Pet 1.9) – something of a Hebrew trait. But Paul is flexible in his imagery, varying his presentation; so he can liken the human person to a seed, first buried in the ground before emerging in very

different guise (1 Cor 15.36-38). As we reach the climax of this passage (15.49), echoes of Philippians 3.21 are heard: "Just as we have borne the image of the man of dust, we shall also bear the image of the man of heaven" i.e. become like Christ. Whereas one might have thought the imagery of seed and plant implied a process of growth (as noted earlier in Christ's teaching about God's kingdom), Paul speaks here of change "in a moment, in the twinkling of an eye" (v52), when the dead will be raised "imperishable".

In 2 Corinthians 4.13-5.10 there is certainly the aspiration, akin to that of Philippians 1.21, of being "away from the body and at home with the Lord"; but this is not explicitly linked to the passage of death. When that occurs (5.1)[94], the imagery this time speaks of being "further clothed" with the life that comes from God (5.4-5). Paul affirms that a "guarantee" (elsewhere called "first fruits") of this has already been experienced in the gift of the Spirit, so he does not envisage sharp discontinuity between this world and the next. If 4.14 ("[*God*] will raise us also with Jesus and bring us with you into his presence") is to be read alongside 5.6 ("while we are at home in the body we are away from the Lord"), it would seem to be his belief here that resurrection brings Christians corporately into the presence of Christ, where his judgment seat (5.10) is then to be faced, albeit with confidence (3.4). "The Lord who is the Spirit" is actively preparing the faithful for that day. "We all, with unveiled face, beholding the glory of the Lord, are being changed into his likeness from one degree of glory to another" (3.18). Once again, the final goal is presented as being "like Christ".

Confidence is evident too in Romans, written not many months later than 2 Corinthians. Paul speaks of "the glorious liberty of the children of God" (Rom 8.21), a new relationship entered through baptism "into Christ" (6.3). Paul often refers to this existential bond as being "in Christ", which here implies that the believer has already been "buried" with him (v4), and hence has a certain hope of being "united with him in a resurrection like his" (v5 cf Jn 11.25). He adds later though that "each of us shall give due account of himself" (14.12) before God's (*not Christ's*) judgment seat. But in both life and death, he insists, "we are the Lord's" (14.8). Death and what lies beyond it are plainly not to be feared, because "none of us dies to himself ... if we die, we die to the Lord". But "life from the dead" (11.15) has a definite future aspect, if only because the work of salvation has yet to include Paul's fellow Jews (v14). In 2 Timothy, whether by Paul or (more likely, in view of the less Christocentric language) by one of his followers, there is a note of eager

---

[94] Death is the destruction of our "earthly tent", a rare reference to his trade, in which Paul admits that his products are by no means guaranteed to last for ever!

anticipation: "Henceforth there is laid up for me the crown of righteousness, which the Lord, the righteous judge will award me on that day, and not only to me but to also to all who have loved his appearing" (4.8).

What of the Johannine tradition? In the fourth gospel there is the promise to the disciples that they will "follow" where Jesus leads the way (Jn 13.36). He is in fact "leaving the world and going to the Father" (16.28), where he will "prepare a place" (14.2-3). Such *monai* (abiding places) feature also in 1 and 2 Enoch, but here are otherwise unspecified. St. Augustine's comment on Jesus' work of "preparation" is particularly apt, viz. that it is done by Jesus preparing those who believe in him. This is at least partially realised in the promise of 14.23: "If a man loves me, he will keep my word, and my Father will love him, and we will come to him and make our home [*abide*] with him". Similarly (although with less emphasis[95] now upon the person of Christ), in the Johannine letters there is the further assurance: "if we love one another, God abides in us and his love is perfected in us" (1 Jn 4.12). Since "he who abides in love abides in God, and God abides in him" (v16), "we may have confidence for the day of judgment" (v17).

In the book of Revelation, it is the Christian martyrs who form the vanguard[96]. By way of comparison, Hebrews 12.23 seems to include with them the heroes of the faith listed in chapter 11 ("the spirits of just men made perfect"), having made clear earlier that Christ "by a single offering …perfected for all time those who are sanctified" (Heb 10.14 cf 2.10). Such as these have a place in heaven already (Rev 6.9), wearing white robes (v11) of perfection and victory. But they must await others, such as the "witnesses" (11.3) who are still suffering in Christ's name, before coming fully to life (20.4). For the time being, they are resting from their labours (14.13). "Over such the second death has no power" (20.6), hence they have nothing to fear at the last judgment, and so may be described as already reigning with Christ (vv4,6). It is worth noting that in his final vision the Seer remains true to the Johannine understanding of God's abiding presence with his people. Not only is the new Jerusalem seen as "coming down" (Rev 3.12; 21.2,10), but God himself dwells in it (21.3). Rev 21.22 may in fact be understood as the

---

[95] The elder testifies to "the message" of Christ (1 Jn 1.5; 3.11), whereas in the fourth gospel Christ is the very *Logos* himself.
[96] The interpretation of the "twenty four elders" around God's throne (Rev 4.4) varies. More in line with Hebrews, these could be the twelve patriarchs of the Old Testament in company with the twelve apostles, drawing together the two covenants of God's people; or they may symbolise the heavenly court encountered in the Old Testament (above, 3.4).

ultimate fulfilment of Jesus' prophecy about the temple[97] in John 3.19; 4.20ff. As Christ's risen body replaced his earthly body, which was seen no more, so the holy city ("prepared for them" by God in Heb 11.16) has now replaced whatever was once on earth, which has "passed away" (Rev 21.1-4). Here again there is a parallel in Hebrews: "Now he has promised, Yet once more I will shake not only the earth but also the heaven" (12.26). This, we read, "indicates the removal of what is shaken, as of what has been made, in order that what cannot be shaken may remain. Therefore let us be grateful for receiving a kingdom that cannot be shaken" (12.27-28).

So what is the Christian's hope? Brief mention may be made here about the well-established concept of "the book of life", found even in non-Biblical sources. Its history certainly stretches back to Moses, who requests God to forgive his people "and if not, blot me, I pray thee, out of the book which thou hast written" (Ex 32.32). Malachi 3.16 speaks of "a book of remembrance ... of those who feared the Lord and thought on his name"; while it is Daniel 7.10; 12.1 which look to the day when such books were to be opened. Jesus himself urges his disciples not to celebrate their achievements so much as to "rejoice that your names are written in heaven" (Lk 10.20). Paul mentions "the book of life" in Philippians 4.3; and as noted earlier there are those who are "enrolled in heaven" in Hebrews 12.23. But it is John the Seer who makes most reference to it (Rev 3.5; 17.8; 20.12,15), naming also "the Lamb's book of life" (13.8; 21.27), which may be the same as the "other" book of 20.12. While the former texts appear to refer to God's record of persons and their deeds (a book of remembrance, as in Ps 56.8), the Lamb's book must surely witness to the saving work of Christ, and so to the wider embrace of God's mercy and forgiveness. According to Colossians 2.14, "the bond" or record (NRSV) which stood against us was cancelled when - metaphorically - it was nailed to the cross. Hence the faithful who turn to Christ, as emphasised across the New Testament, need "have no anxiety" (Phil 4.6) so long as hearts and minds remain "in Christ Jesus" (v7). "For life is to be with Christ; where Christ is, there is life, there is the kingdom" (St. Ambrose of Milan). Nor is death is to be feared, for it is Christ who holds "the keys of death and Hades" (Rev 1.18). While St. Ignatius of Antioch awaited his martyrdom, therefore, his thoughts turned to the life that lay beyond it: "the birth pangs are upon me".

Heavenly Realities

---

[97] Compare Paul's description of the human person as God's temple, indwelt by the Holy Spirit (1 Cor 3.16f; 6.19).

During the years of apartheid in South Africa, the one-time Anglican dean of Johannesburg, Gonville ffrench-Beytagh, was arrested for his active opposition, and during some of his time in prison was kept in solitary confinement. He was allowed virtually nothing in his cell, but could not of course be prevented from saying his prayers. He recounts how he would continue to offer mass, using perhaps bread and water, and relying on his memory for Bible passages and the consecration prayer. His testimony is that the spiritual world came alive for him then far more than he had ever experienced in his cathedral church, with acolytes and candles, with the choir and organ, and a large congregation sounding their responses, with vestments, ceremonial and clouds of incense. Rather it was here, in his apparent isolation, that he was conscious of being surrounded by a cloud of witnesses, the company of saints, the angels and all the hosts of heaven (cf Heb 12.22). This matches exactly the experience of John in his exile on Patmos, who was "in the Spirit on the Lord's day" (Rev 1.10), and one not wholly dissimilar from Isaiah's vision centuries earlier (Isa 6.1ff).

We may be reminded of the episode recorded in 2 Kings 6.8ff, where the prophet Elisha found himself in a heavily besieged city, with a servant terrified at the prospect. "Fear not," is Elisha's response, "for those who are with us are more than those who are with them." Then Elisha prayed, and said, "O Lord, I pray thee, open his eyes that he may see." So the Lord opened the eyes of the young man, and he saw; "and behold, the mountain was full of horses and chariots of fire round about Elisha." Similar angelic protection is found in the story of the burning fiery furnace (Dan 3.19ff), in which the three young Jews are joined by a fourth person. "Did we not cast three men bound into the fire?" They answered the king, "True, king." He answered, "But I see four men loose, walking in the midst of the fire, and they are not hurt; and the appearance of the fourth is like a son of the gods."

So by one means or another God is able to reassure his people both of his immediate presence, not least in an hour of danger, and also of a more glorious future in his company. Paul mentions in 2 Corinthians 12 what is apparently (v7) his own ecstasy, when he "was caught up into paradise - whether in the body or out of the body I do not know, God knows - and he heard things that cannot be told, which man may not utter" (vv3-4). Angels if "seen" - and of course this can only be in a vision, or perhaps a dream, for they are not physical entities[98] - are among God's messengers, whose role is

---

[98] This creates representational problems for artists: the earlier symbolism of the halo, dating back to the 5th century AD, gave place to the greater naturalism of

to awaken us to spiritual realities (Heb 1.14). Usually they are "heard" i.e. their voices sound "in the head" (as St. Joan explained patiently to her inquisitors in Bernard Shaw's play of that name). They appear giving guidance, for example, to Joseph (Mt 1.20; 2.13,19,22); to Zechariah (Lk 1.11); to Mary (Lk 1.26); to Cornelius (Acts 10.3); to Peter (Acts 10.14; 12.7). At other times, they sing God's praises, especially "new" songs which celebrate Christ's human birth and his work of salvation (e.g. Lk 2.13; Rev 5.9-10). Hence they assist in the Church's eucharistic offering: in the words of the Anglican *anaphora*, "therefore with angels and archangels, and with all the company of heaven, we laud and magnify thy glorious name". Paul seems to suggest that the gift of glossolalia may perhaps sound like "the tongues" of angels (1 Cor 13.1). But he knows that "the heathen" may be moved in the presence of "dumb idols" (12.2) to ecstatic utterances also, which may be either meaningless or worse, so insists that God's communications are always purposeful and salvific, speaking above all of love.

Other cautionary words are not out of place here. There is a warning by Paul, or by one of his followers, about visions, on which some misguidedly take their "stand" (Col 2.18). These false teachers, full of "empty deceit" (v8) - and indeed conceit (v18) - insist on "worship of angels", which perhaps implies some mystical experience in which the person of Christ is sidelined. Clearly there was a real danger at times that angelology could get out of hand, which may be why Hebrews 1.4 stresses the "superiority" of Christ, who only "for a little while was made lower than the angels" (2.9). 1 Peter 1.12 underlines that it is Christians who have received tidings, "into which angels long to look". Angels are also ignorant of the timing of "that day" (Mt 24.36) and are certainly not to be worshipped (Rev 19.10; 22.8-9). Indeed (as noted above, 4.1), according to Paul they are one day to be "judged" by the faithful, and his rhetoric in Romans 8.38 allows for at least the possibility that they may somehow attempt to come between Christians and their Lord.

Yet theirs is an important and valid ministry, however it may be abused. Angels "minister" to Jesus in the wilderness (Mk 1.13 cf Mt 4.11), a phrase omitted by Luke, who was perhaps not therefore responsible for depicting "an angel from heaven, strengthening" Jesus in Gethsemane (Lk 22.43 in some, but not all, ancient manuscripts). And we are assured that "little ones" (Mt 18.10 i.e. Christian disciples) have their guardian angels, as also (according to Rev 1.20) do the Christian churches. In the words of St. Basil of Caesarea, "Beside each believer stands an angel as protector and shepherd leading him to life"; or, as St. Bernard of Clairvaux expressed it, "Heaven denies us

---

Renaissance art, until an "emanation of light" became the standard Baroque feature.

nothing that assists us", hence "these celestial spirits have been placed at our sides to protect us, instruct us and to guide us".

Testimony to the reality of this protection is found widely across the Christian Church at times of particular danger[99] or persecution. In Malawi, during the dictatorial rule of Dr. Kamuzu Banda which ended only in 1994, an Irish missionary Jack Selfridge has recorded how when Banda's Young Pioneers were on a rampage of terror, Christians who had taken refuge in a church building became collectively conscious of an angelic host surrounding the building. The Young Pioneers approached, but were turned away - evidently by spiritual forces that thwarted their evil intentions. During the same period other such episodes were experienced elsewhere in Malawi. It may be relevant to observe that Selfridge's background was Celtic, and that in that tradition angelic protection plays a significant role: "I bind unto myself the power / of the great love of cherubim; / ... / the service of the seraphim" are words from the enduring "St. Patrick's breastplate" (although probably to be ascribed to the 8th century St. Fursa). This *lorica* prayer in its fullest version (certainly relevant to Patrick's own earlier struggle on Tara with witches and pagan druids) asks for protection against "Satan's spells and wiles", as also against "the wizard's evil craft". Many similar prayers were produced at this time by the Irish Church, some of which[100] are recorded in the *Carmina Gadelica* made by Alexander Carmichael in the early 20th century. The words were often accompanied by symbolic action: the index finger of the right hand would draw an encompassing circle around the believer, as a reminder of God's embracing presence and his protecting angels. It is of interest to see this depicted artistically too; on the ancient cross of Kells, Daniel may be seen between two lions, holding out his arms in prefiguration of Christ, while the three young men are to be found in the fiery furnace sheltering under the wings of an angel. Early Irish homilies spoke frequently about the conflict between the dark and the bright angels, not least at the moment of death or when a soul was *in extremis*. In a very different tradition one may note the recently canonized Padre Pio da Pietralcina, the Franciscan mystic and stigmatic who died in 1968; in his struggles with demonic powers his peasant earthiness found succour in the guardian angel he

---

[99] New York fireman Bob Peters, in his own view, only survived the events of 11th September 2001 because his guardian angel allowed him to oversleep.

[100] There are prayers for different daily circumstances: for example, "I will kindle my fire this morning in the presence of the holy angels of heaven. God kindle thou in my heart within a flame of love to my neighbour, to my foe, to my friend, to my kindred all, to the brave, to the knave, to the thrall".

referred to familiarly as "my boy"!

There are still entire societies where belief in demons and other forces of evil is rife, and here the Christian response must always be to affirm the presence and protection of God in the company of his heavenly host[101], together with (and despite appearances at times to the contrary) the assured triumph of Christ's victory over whatever is opposed to goodness and truth. "God is faithful, and he will not let you be tempted beyond your strength, but with the temptation will also provide the way of escape, that you may be able to endure it" (1 Cor 10.13). The context here is that of succumbing to the social and religious *mores* of contemporary society, but the principle is even wider, as Paul illustrates later in 2 Corinthians 6.9: "as dying, and behold we live; as punished, and yet not killed; as sorrowful, yet always rejoicing" When Christians feel threatened, Jesus' advice is, "look up and raise your heads, because your redemption is drawing near" (Lk 21.28). Above us, as the Bible often mentions, are the clouds: for some they are signs of God's majesty and power (Ps 68.4), for others their diffused light may point to Christ who radiates his glory (Mk 13.26), while yet again they may be reminders of "so great a cloud of witnesses" (Heb 12.1) who surround the Church on earth. It is these last, including the saints who now exercise a priestly ministry with Christ (Rev 1.6; 20.6), offering their prayers up like incense (Rev 5.8), along with the angels who remind us of God's favour and blessing (Lk 1.28), who may uplift the fearful in whatever place on earth, challenge their doubts, and point them to the source of grace: Christ's own personal presence.

Paul, in 1 Corinthians 4.1, speaks of the Church as steward "of the mysteries of God". The apostolic generation came rapidly to appreciate that they participated in the fruits of redemption above all in "the breaking of the bread" (Acts 2.42). Here they were able to focus upon the significance of Christ's gift of himself for the life of the world, to "remember" and "proclaim" it (1 Cor 11.25-26) in terms of sacrificial offering. Jesus had certainly continued the prophetic criticism of merely ritual observance: "Go

---

[101] The new *Directory of Popular Piety and Liturgy* launched by the Vatican in April 2002 has however reduced the number of archangels to the three with Biblical credentials: Michael, Gabriel and Raphael. It warns against succumbing to a "childish" fatalism, which renounces personal commitment and prayer in favour of seeing the whole of life taken over by cosmological struggles between good and evil. It is curious that modern art and sculpture has found a new fascination with angels, as have some New Age cults – but without the detailed angelology that found expression in the 5th century document *Celestial Hierarchies* by Pseudo-Dionysius.

and learn what this means: I desire mercy and not sacrifice" (Mt 9.13; 12.7 quoting Hos 6.6). But he then described his own death in words alluding to the blood-shedding that sealed Moses' covenant with God: "This cup which is poured out for you is the new covenant in my blood" (Lk 22.20). Again, while the letter to the Hebrews emphatically rejects the former temple dispensation, its author describes it as "a shadow of the good things to come" (10.1), truly efficacious in removing sin (9.27). Paul too sees Christ's death as the "sacrifice" of a paschal lamb (1 Cor 5.7), but also as "an expiation" by his blood (Rom 3.25 cf 1 Jn 1.7; 1 Pet 1.19). The Greek word used is *hilasterion,* which is the mercy seat that once covered the ark of the covenant (Ex 25.17-22), sprinkled with blood in the cleansing rites of the Day of Atonement (Lev 16.15). Hebrews 4.16 sees this mercy seat as "the throne of grace", where Jesus as the true High Priest is to be found (v14), having "passed through the heavens" and entered the Holy of Holies - that is, God's very presence - with his own self-offering.

Ritual therefore retains a central place in the life of the Church, above all in the eucharist, where the emphasis comes to rest upon Christ's gift of his person: "He who eats my flesh and drinks my blood abides in me, and I in him" (Jn 6.56 cf 1 Cor 10.16-17). The terminology has been personalised by Jesus himself. "Bread" is now " his body" or "his flesh", and "cup" has become "his blood": hence ritual is no longer mere performance nor even remembrance, but among all the channels of grace the one in which Christ himself meets the believer at the point of his deepest need. In Christian sacramental practice he is no mere assisting angel, but that "fourth man" - indeed the Son of God - whose presence alongside us in the furnace of our experience delivers us both from the harm we cause ourselves and also from the flames that others may stoke against us. In the famous words of Pope Leo I, "What was present in the Lord has passed into the mysteries"; or with St. Ambrose we may say, "O God, not by mirrors and enigmas but face to face have you revealed yourself to me, and I find you in your mysteries." John 6.52-58 prompts us also to describe this sacramental process in terms of feeding: "My flesh is food indeed ... he who eats this bread will live for ever." No doubt the several experiences of meeting the risen Lord in celebratory meals (Lk 24.30-31,42-43; Jn 21.12-14) endorsed this perspective, giving rise in time to daily celebrations so that the Christian community could ingest "the medicine of immortality".

Humanly speaking, the eucharist (as with each of the Church's sacraments) can answer our needs holistically in a way that other rites, prayers or blessings may often fail to do. Our senses as well as our minds are engaged in the pageantry of ceremonial, in the beauty of chant, in rhythm and dance, in the familiar repetition of responses, in the sounding of bells, drums or other instruments, in gestures that are individual or corporate, in encountering both friends and strangers; but above all of course in receiving the consecrated elements. And holy communion here is also "phatic" communion, that is, the reaffirming of relationships, both human and divine, without any attempt to make personal gain or to resolve personal difficulties. In fact here is a defining distinction between Christian faith and "natural" religion: the latter may be practised, as may recourse to magic, to achieve some advantage or to avert some real or anticipated curse, but Christianity is above all a grateful response to a loving God. In this respect, the Christian's immediate concern may well be less about changing the world around him than about being changed himself. The Church invokes the Holy Spirit as well to challenge the faithful as to equip and strengthen them. Or again, we must reflect that eucharistic reception is not to make Christ serve our purposes but rather to enable us to be at his disposal: not to bring him down to earth, but to raise us up to heaven. After the *sursum corda*, the eucharistic prayer continues: "It is very meet, right, and our bounden duty, that we should at all times, and in all places, give thanks unto thee, O Lord", as if the choruses of heavenly praise in Revelation resound wherever and in whatever state we find ourselves - "as sorrowful, yet always rejoicing; as poor, yet making many rich; as having nothing, and yet possessing everything" (2 Cor 6.10).

When James, however, looks around at the Christians of his day, he observes serious shortcomings between the actual and the ideal. He sees the inconsistency with which, on the one hand, we bless God, and, on the other, we curse our fellow human beings, who are made in God's likeness: "From the same mouth come blessing and cursing. My brethren, this ought not to be so" (Jas 3.10). Paul is sure that this "natural" state of affairs is overridden in Christ. "Bless those who persecute you; bless and do not curse them" (Rom 12.14, echoing Jesus in Mt 5.11,44); for, he insists, Christ has redeemed us from the law of cursing, retribution and revenge, "having become a curse for us" (Gal 3.13). Wherever Christians find themselves, there is to be a profound sense of gratitude which overflows in blessings to all around, "for the former things have passed away" (Rev 21.4). We are, in Christ and in company with heaven, a eucharistic people; and as such are called to be ourselves a sacrament, or sign, of heavenly realities in the places where we live.

Chapter 5

Boundaries of Belief

The Riches of God's Glory

Paul, who to the weak "became weak" (1 Cor 9.22), that he might win the weak "for the sake of the gospel" (v23) would surely continue that policy in today's world, where as ever there is much human weakness and need. In particular, there are the stresses and fears manifested in different cultures, sometimes more marked in one society than in another. The Church's response, thanks to the varied language and insights of the Bible, can often be particularised accordingly. "The riches" of God's glory (Rom 9.23; 11.33 cf Eph 3.8), which are also "the treasures of wisdom and knowledge" (Col 2.3), allow us to express the faith appropriately, in ways as differentiated as Paul's. His thought is not easily systematised, but is full of explosive ideas and creative language to bring home the truth of God's mystery, "which is Christ in you, the hope of glory" (Col 1.27). Indeed, as Basil of Caesarea remarked (in *Concerning Faith*), the things of God "cannot be defined in language nor comprehended by human intellect", nor grasped in any partial concepts, but require "a variety of speech". There is a richness too in the very plurality of the New Testament canon, and yet at times schools of interpretation, or of theological fashion, have seemed blind to some aspects of it. The experience of living in Central Africa has made me realise a few at least of my own prejudices and blind spots, opening my eyes to the reality of the spiritual world portrayed in the Bible. There have also been times in the past when one scriptural writing or another has passed out of favour. Thus, Marcion took a narrow viewpoint in selecting his permitted texts, while others excluded perhaps only those of latest origin, Eusebius describing them as "disputed" works. Luther would have none of James, while Calvin gave the least attention to Revelation. Many even now would readily jettison Leviticus. But Leviticus continues to motivate the Jubilee campaign for debt remission. James likewise is firmly reinstated, and valued for its trenchant criticism of injustice (even within the Church). Revelation has some of the profoundest glimpses into heaven, both reflecting and inspiring Christian worship. And the Old Testament as a whole is seen to cover an even broader range of human experience, with little of the pietism that can so easily infect religion, than is found in the New Testament.

Today, as suggested earlier (4.1), the materialism of science, which strongly influenced the basic assumptions of many 20th century Bible scholars (most famously, Bultmann and those who with him would "demythologise" the text), has given place to a more speculative cosmology, as mathematical physics has discovered a multiplicity[102] of other possible solutions of its equations, suggesting, theoretically at least (for there is always a gap between the potential and the actual), the existence of other worlds. Even within this universe, many now hold that sentient beings may have evolved or emerged in other galaxies. A less doctrinaire approach to the Bible has therefore become possible, with more sympathetic respect for the miraculous and the supranormal. Within this philosophical shift, the rehabilitation of the spirit world, including the saints in glory and the angelic host, seems overdue, provided this can be understood within a critical Christian perspective. There are, it will be recalled, caveats within the New Testament itself (e.g. 1 Jn 4.1) that must be properly heeded. While the main thrust of these foundational documents is a positive proclamation of the gospel, inevitably they include also serious warnings about distortions of the faith (e.g. 2 Pet 3.16), malpractices, and their consequences. There are certainly "godless and silly myths" (1 Tim 4.7 cf Tit 1.14), as well as misleading teachings often put about by self-appointed Messiahs (Mk 13.6,22). Such are described as false prophets disguised "in sheep's clothing, but inwardly they are ravenous wolves" (Mt 7.15 cf Jn 10.12).

It is clear, for example, that no quarter is given in the New Testament to magicians, sorcerers and the like. The magi's visit to Jesus in Mt 2 may be seen as their act of homage, and it is possible to detect in Revelation 21 a coded attack upon astrology: the jewels adorning the new Jerusalem (vv 19-20 cf Ex 28.17-20) were noted by R.H. Charles to be those symbolising the zodiac - but in reverse order! This may strike some as scholarship running to excess, but it is certainly true that all classes of Mediterranean society were given to astrological speculations at this time. Paul believed that many were enslaved by *stoicheia* (Gal 4.9) i.e. demonic or astral forces, prior to their Christian conversion. "Horoscopes were avidly compiled and interpreted. The most important deity to the ordinary mortal was not Zeus but Chance (Tyche) or Fate. This was the power who ended life, and from whose thralldom salvation must be sought."[103] Frend cites here the words of Seneca writing in 60 AD to his friend Marcia: portraying the journey of her dead

---

[102] Of course, further exploration may discover previously unrealised boundary conditions which reduce this multiplicity significantly.
[103] W.H.C.Frend: *The Early Church (Philadelphia, 1982)*

child's soul through the stars, he noted how "on even the slightest motion of these hang the fortunes of nations, and the greatest and smallest events are shaped to accord with the progress of a kindly or unkindly star". The pervasiveness of such beliefs may be judged by the discovery of horoscopes even in the caves at Qumran, where fragments have been dated to the late 1st century BC. Thus, cave 4 yielded up the following astrological physiognomy: "His thighs are long and lean, and his toes are thin and long. He is of the second column. His spirit consists of six parts in the House of Light and three in the Pit of Darkness. And this is his birthday on which he is to be born: in the foot of the Bull. He will be meek. And his animal is the bull."[104] Of course, many Jews frowned upon astrology, but others, such as the Hellenistic writer Eupolemus, were prepared to credit its earliest use to Abraham.

Whatever contemporary pagans or Jews may have thought, there is no breath of assimilation nor any compromise within the Christian canon. It was reckoned necessary for Simon the magician to be challenged and converted (by stages) in Samaria (Acts 8.9ff), and for Bar-Jesus or Elymas mentioned in the retinue of the proconsul of Cyprus as a (Jewish) magician to be attacked by Paul as a fraud. We may note too how in Thyatira Paul exorcises a spirit of divination in a slave girl, used by her owners as a source of income; and how occult practices are confessed by believers in Ephesus, many of whom came together to burn their books of magic - an indication of the heightened levels of superstition at this time. St. Ignatius of Antioch reminded the Ephesians later, "Christ has dissolved all magic". So sorcery is firmly condemned by Paul in his letters (Gal 5.20)[105] as "a work of the flesh", excluding its practitioners from God's kingdom, along with those who worship demons (1 Cor 6.9). He offers a fuller analysis in Romans 1; by these and other evil practices, he argues, God's given order is turned upside down. People "exchange" (vv23,25,26) what he has granted for distortions and follies of their own devising, so that "the creature" (ultimately their own desires) is served "rather than the creator" (v25). God's response is to "give them up" (vv24,26,28) to face the inevitable consequences. Where wrong-doing in some New Testament writings clearly results in punishment imposed from without (e.g. the fate of sorcerers in Rev 21.8), and much is made of Hades (e.g. Mt 11.23) and even more of Gehenna (e.g. Mk 9.43; Jas 3.6) with its "unquenchable fire", Paul sees both rewards and penalties in largely intrinsic terms. His hope is not to gain any extra heavenly blessing, beyond

---

[104] G.Vermes: *The Complete Dead Sea Scrolls (Harmondsworth, 1997)*

[105] One may also note Paul's rhetorical question, "Who has bewitched you?" (Gal 3.1)

being "with Christ" more closely (Phil 1.23); which implies that to part company with God is the ultimate fate. John likewise stresses that the hour for responding to the Son is "now", and that "those who hear will live" (Jn 5.25); which again carries the implication that those who fail to do this, such as sorcerers, having deprived themselves of God's presence will be among those left outside the holy city (Rev 22.15).

There are thus boundaries of belief, which every so often may need further demarcation[106]. Yet otherwise, within the expressions of the Christian faith canonised in these early witnesses, there is considerable latitude for different emphases, according to time and place. The 2nd Vatican Council Decree on Ecumenism (*Unitatis Redintegratio, 1964*) offers this wise advice: "In Catholic teaching there exists an order or 'hierarchy' of truths, since they vary in their relationship to the foundation of the Christian faith. Thus the way will be opened ... to incite all to a deeper realization and a clearer expression of the unfathomable riches of Christ". Frend (*op cit*) gives an example from the 4th century of two quite different, but authentic, expressions of Christian spirituality, contrasting two pillars of doctrinal orthodoxy viz. Athanasius of Alexandria and Basil of Caesarea. The former "had tended to envisage salvation in physical terms – of salvation from death and destruction through the overthrow of demonic powers. These, as he shows in his *Life of Antony*, were stark realities to him, as they were to nearly every other Egyptian of the age... Heaven could only be won by a soul infused with divine power through Christ, and to possess that divine power Christ must be fully God. But demonology has little or no part in Basil's thought. Instead, we find (as in Origen) the spiritual aim of raising the human soul stage by stage toward the divine goodness, which was God. Blessedness, to Basil, as later to Augustine, was the soul's rest in God. Evil was represented not so much by demonic powers as by the simple lack of goodness... Man, made in the image of God, had the means of increasing the intensity of his likeness through the saving work of Jesus Christ." Once again, this could only be achieved if Christ himself was fully of "the same essence" as the Father. Given such adherence to Christian fundamentals, it is surely possible for churches today, as well as in the 4th century, to find their own *via media* in a particular cultural setting. This will require much attention being given to the spiritual realities which can both uplift and threaten people: for where this fails to happen, recourse is

---

[106] Another critical period for the Church was in the 2nd century when Gnostic teachers began to elaborate ever more complex spiritual hierarchies, denying the efficacy of Christ's earthly life and death by ascribing to him only the power of spiritual illumination.

readily made to alternative practitioners, seducing the gullible and confusing even the faithful.

There is one remarkable church in Africa which has a longer history of inculturation than any other, and may therefore usefully illustrate some of the possibilities. The Ethiopian Orthodox Church has never neglected its Biblical inheritance, incorporating a rich sacramental life. But neither has it failed to accommodate traditional views of the spirit world, offering the faithful protection against malevolence in ways that correspond to their understanding and experience. Although Christianity spread across Egypt and North Africa during the first three centuries, it was in the next century that it reached the hinterland. The story is told of two Christian boys from Syria captured and enslaved at the court of the powerful kingdom of Aksum, in the mountainous region north of the rift valley. However, having made converts to the faith, including King Ezana who ascribed some of his successes to this benign influence, one of the two, Frumentius, went in 346 to consult St. Athanasius, Patriarch of Alexandria, about the future needs of the burgeoning Christian community. He found himself consecrated bishop, or *abuna*, and challenged to adapt the practices of the church to the culture of the Amharic people. The Coptic right to appoint the *abuna* (invariably an Egyptian) for the Ethiopian Orthodox Church continued, with occasional interruptions, until 1948, and might have led in the opposite direction viz. the imposition of foreign customs upon the people. In fact, such insensitivity was displayed only for a brief period in the early 17th century, when, for political reasons, Jesuits from Portugal held the supreme office and attempted (but failed) to make reforms in a stridently Catholic direction. Relations with the Church of Rome are nonetheless in good shape today. "When the Venerable Patriarch of the Ethiopian Church, Abuna Paulos, paid me a visit in Rome on 11th June 1993, together we emphasized the deep communion existing between our two Churches: 'We share the faith handed down from the Apostles, as also the same sacraments and the same ministry, rooted in the apostolic succession. Today, moreover, we can affirm that we have the one faith in Christ, even though for a long time this was a source of division between us'.[107]

Apart from the *abuna*, priests and deacons were largely drawn from peasant families, with certain hereditary rights, but who lacked the learning which flourished in the many monasteries (a characteristic feature of Coptic Christianity, dating back to St. Antony). In practice the liturgical life of parishes depended much more on educated lay-men, known as *debtera*, who received thorough initiation into the wealth of ancient chants (deriving from

---

[107] John Paul II: *Ut Unum Sint (Vatican, 1995)*

the 6th century St. Yared, who also introduced the use of drums, dancing and the *sistrum* or rattle), but who often had considerable skills also as healers, drawing upon the spiritual assistance of a host of saints and angels, particularly the Blessed Virgin Mary (honoured in the *Weddase Maryam* which follows the Ethiopian Psalter and contains Marian hymns and prayers for each day of the week), St. George, the archangels Michael and Gabriel (invariably flanking Mary in the many frescoes, each remembered on a monthly basis in the calendar), along with lesser known local saints. This protective cult continues today, together with the observance of a full round of festivals and fasts. Many of the saints are thought to have tamed or vanquished dangerous animals, in whom demons commonly find themselves a home. Their exploits are frequently recorded in medieval miracle writings, and have given rise to the Ethiopian idea of the *kidran mehret*, or covenant of mercy, by which the saints have been granted power by Christ to intervene in favour of afflicted sinners, provided the latter can claim at least one good deed.

Belief in demons, as it happens, increased rapidly in the 19th century as areas to the south of the old Amharic empire were Christianised. There was perhaps too great a readiness to assimilate elements from tribal cultures, which - in the absence of theologically well-trained pastors - meant that some less desirable beliefs and ideas have taken root within the church as well. Thus, while witchcraft itself is not greatly in evidence, there is much fear of those thought to be "possessed", and misfortune is readily ascribed to "the evil eye". *Debteras* are given to the production of magic parchment rolls and other charms to ward off evil forces: amulets are sown into a red case and worn about the body, while most churches also offer holy water and healing earth known as *emnet* (literally "faith"). Social tensions exist too between certain castes of society, who by means of taboos and other restrictions maintain a distance from one another. The Ethiopian experiment is not therefore without its own flaws and weaknesses, but much of value can be learnt from its history.

Indeed, churches elsewhere in the continent (e.g. in South Africa, starting in the Rand in 1892) have more recently taken pride in this African version of Christianity (partly because of its inherent political inspiration viz. "Africa for the Africans") and have imitated some of its features i.e. its adaptation to African customs and beliefs. Legio Maria is the largest independent Catholic church in sub-Saharan Africa, combining the Latin mass and Catholic ritual with a range of popular charismatic experiences: healing, exorcism, witchcraft negation and removal, prophecy, glossolalia, dream interpretation and visions, meeting a demand for specific prayers and blessings. Again, Dinis Sengulane, Anglican Bishop of Lebombo in Mozambique, has written: "When liturgy takes into account children, the young, adults, the old, the departed, spiritual beings (whether regarded as angels or demons), rain and environment, national leaders, heaven and hell, houses and fields, colour and movement, gestures and symbols, then it is dealing with what concerns African peoples, as it builds up the worship of God, Father, Son, and Holy Spirit."[108]   Others (especially the stricter Protestant churches) are uneasy about what appears to them here to be bordering upon syncretism. But, as I have tried to indicate, there is in the Bible already a wholesome syncretism[109], where much has been learnt, with its truth or otherwise being carefully sifted, about the invisible world of spirits, whether beneficent or the opposite; about the relationship between the living and the departed; about the hosts of heaven, the saints and angels; and about God's sovereignty over all this realm, including his chosen means of redemption as of grace. Western or missionary churches have at times overlooked some of this spiritual treasury, although admittedly at the other extreme there are churches which have accepted indigenous beliefs and practices uncritically i.e. without relating them to the central truths[110] of the faith.

The need remains, however, across the world for a Christianity that is more responsive to people's felt needs and actual circumstances. John Paul II in *Redemptoris Missio (1990)* reminded the Church that this is no new issue. The New Testament itself actually records a similar debate at the Council of Jerusalem (48 AD), where in Acts 15 it was resolved that (in his words): "From now on the Church opens her doors and becomes the house which all may enter, and in which all can feel at home, while keeping their own culture and traditions, *provided* these are not contrary to the Gospel."

The Spirit of Truth

Whereas at times in the past the Christian Church may have propagated its

---

[108] Dinis Sengulane: *An African Perspective (London, 1991)*
[109] Adolf von Harnack stressed this in the 1920s, seeing in the Christian faith a capacity to include "elements from other cultures and religions", and hence a potential universalism.
[110] Above all there is the "one thing" commended by Jesus in his conversation with Mary and Martha as needful (Lk 10.42); among the Christian's many and varied resources in his daily struggles not least is his (or her) relationship to Christ himself, the fount of life and hope.

beliefs in a triumphalist manner, ready to ride roughshod over the cherished values that other peoples may have held, the past half-century has seen much contrition for such intransigent attitudes and a determination to approach different cultures with greater respect. One of the milestones in this change of heart was the 2nd Vatican Council, held during the early 1960s, although this was not reached unquestioningly. There was, for example, a very significant debate in preparing *Gaudium et Spes*, or "Pastoral Constitution of the Church in the Modern World". Initial drafting proposed a much greater openness towards the work of the Holy Spirit in the world at large, but this was subsequently toned down after criticism from German-speaking theologians. Karl Rahner spoke of "the antagonism between a world under the power of the Evil One and the disciples of Christ" that "will never be mitigated but will grow ever more bitter in the course of time". Joseph Ratzinger likewise found the draft too much focused upon the incarnation; "an orientation of the Church towards the world which would mean turning away from the Cross would not lead to a renewal of the Church, but to its decline and eventual decay."

Nevertheless, the Council's thinking did undergo certain shifts. One of the shorter, yet certainly seminal, documents that emerged was *Nostra Aetate*, or "Declaration on the relationship of the Church to non-Christian religions". Its second chapter reflects that "From ancient times down to the present, there has existed among diverse peoples a certain perception of that hidden power which hovers over the course of things and over the events of human life". Christian faith and occult practice are different responses to this power. Some, such as sorcerers, seek to use it in harmful ways, to gain advantage for themselves or their clients. Others, *sing'anga* among them, attempt to tame its protective or its healing properties. Others yet again, including Christians, sense that this mysterious power is not to be exploited, but - having a transcendent nature - has the capacity to lift us above ourselves into a new dimension of life altogether. Here the prayer of faith, rather than the incantation of magic, seems the appropriate way forward.

The same document, *Nostra Aetate*, continues: "The Catholic Church rejects nothing which is true and holy ... She looks with sincere respect upon those ways of conduct and of life, those rules and teachings which, though differing in many particulars from what she holds and sets forth, nevertheless often reflect a ray of that Truth which enlightens all men". This sets the tone for the whole process of inculturation, which certainly implies that within the unity of the Christian faith there is legitimate diversity of expression. Further, any "way of life and conduct" necessarily presupposes a certain framework of ideas, so that in so far as a particular culture is compatible with Christianity, it will also reflect particular theological emphases. It has already been noted (above, 5.1) that there is a plurality of thought within the Christian canon, as within the Synoptic tradition, the Pauline corpus, and the Johannine writings. This material is not wholly self-consistent, but that does not imply either that it lacks coherence or that its ideas may be exploited without limit. The present paper, sensing that post-modern liberality is reluctant to address this issue, has sought to find parameters within the complex writings of the Bible. What emerges is a steady development of thought - as, for example, over the character of Sheol, the status of the departed, the nature and extent of evil spirits, the efficacy and place of ritual - requiring further deliberation by the Church. Here, however, there is the assurance of guidance, even beyond the patristic period which determined the composition of the New Testament, from the Holy Spirit, who "will teach you all things, and bring to your remembrance all that I have said to you" (Jn 14.26). He is described also as "the Spirit of Truth" who "will bear witness to me [*Jesus*]" (Jn 15.26), which locates Christ himself as God's authoritative expression of truth i.e. as uniquely revelatory. The Spirit's role therefore appears as "educative", drawing out the fuller meanings to be found in Christ himself, rather than to propose inconsistent alternatives. Further, the exercise of discernment in these matters has been entrusted to the Church (Mt 18.18), specifically to that "rock" which Peter represents (16.17-19). In the *Catechism of the Catholic Church (1994)* we therefore read: "Pastoral discernment is needed to sustain and support popular piety and, if necessary, to purify and correct the religious sense which underlies it, so that the faithful may advance in knowledge of the mystery of Christ."

The criterion is above all that of truth, which is not confined to the pages of the Bible. Nor does scripture insist upon this: for example, the Wisdom tradition of the Old Testament was happy to draw upon, and even to include, wisdom sayings from other Near East collections (e.g. Egyptian sayings in Proverbs 22.17-24.22; and from Massa in 30.1-4; 31.1-9), while Paul testifies to the idea of "natural" theology in Romans 1.19; 2.15. Truth, which is indivisible, although at times paradoxical, may also be determined by reason and experience[111] - such as the careful observation of the world and its

---

[111] Cf Paul VI in his encyclical letter *Mysterium Fidei (1965)*: "The Church employs ... concepts which are not tied to any specified cultural system ... They present the perception which the human mind acquires from its universal, essential experience of reality ... They are, therefore, within the reach of everyone at all times and in all places."

workings, sometimes too glibly dismissed as "inappropriate western ideas", but understandably so by those who have never looked through a microscope. Hence, while respecting the way in which belief in magic and the human causation of events function as social mechanisms in non-western societies, these beliefs are not above careful scrutiny, and need to be weighed carefully. A few examples may suffice:

Mwabvi: The Montfort Fathers, who reached Malawi in 1901 and settled in Ngoni territory, very soon encountered the widely practised custom of trial by poison. The following is an extract from their diary[112], on 8th May 1902: "We had known that *mwabvi* was drunk by the inhabitants of surrounding villages, with the exception of the one in which we live. All started when a woman was accused of having made another person die by using her magical arts. And so she had to undergo the test as a result of which she died. It was then decided that everyone should undergo this barbaric ritual, with the result that twenty-five people died. According to tradition, their bodies were not given a decent burial but were thrown into the forest to become the prey of wild beasts. A chief forced his little son to drink the poison and he too died. Often, while they are still alive and in agony, the victims are beaten or stoned. Such is the horror in which those guilty of witchcraft are held". There is overwhelming evidence, of course, that reaction to substances varies greatly with the person, and prescriptions from a pharmacist invariably carry warnings of possible side-effects of differing severity. The nature of such reactions, as of allergies (which play a greater part today in that actual poison is less likely to be used than, say, certain herbs stuffed up the nostrils), is the subject of intense research today, but the moral status of the patient or victim is the least likely factor. However, such a belief system as *mwabvi* does not lack any logical coherence (as is also true of some now outmoded scientific theories) and indeed is "unfalsifiable". It is quite incapable though of proceeding beyond a climate of suspicion to bring conclusive evidence against any particular person at all, unless there are the observable marks of a crime - for which *mwabvi* is then quite superfluous. It is of course (logically) impossible for anyone to defend himself against such a charge. When the outcome is the deaths of so many people, *mwabvi* and all that it represents is certainly found wanting at the bar of justice, and may be described as perniciously false - in fact, in Christian terms as evil because of the slaughter of innocents and the endemic slavery to fear and distrust.

If, however, *mwabvi* is to be roundly condemned, it should not be forgotten that Christian Europe once had similarly mistaken procedures, despite the

---

[112] Cited in L. Nervi: *Malawi - Flames in the African Sky (Balaka, Malawi, 1999)*

desire to bring the transitory affairs of men before some kind of divine tribunal. R.W.Southern[113] has, for example, described the use in medieval times of fasting followed by the reception of the Blessed Sacrament in a water ordeal for suspected criminals. Just as the waters of the Red Sea parted for Moses and the children of Israel, so it was thought they would give way for the innocent, but would reject the guilty. Southern comments: "It were well for a man to sink and hope to be pulled out in time."

Witches: While malevolent people are a fact of life in every society and their curses can have considerable psychological potency, resulting in genuine distress and illness, if not worse, the powers credited to witches again strain credulity. It is claimed that they fly on sticks at night, giving off a grey light; at times becoming invisible; at other times turning themselves into animals or, at least, employing such creatures as cats, dogs, monkeys, birds, toads, beetles as their familiars. (Comparisons with bizarre Biblical imagery fall down as soon as its symbolic character is appreciated.) They or their familiars, who may include very small people too, then carry out their destructive work - ruining crops, eating corpses, setting houses on fire, poisoning food and water, killing both cattle and people (whose nail parings, hair, skin, or even footprints have been obtained for this purpose). They force others to labour for them, hoeing their fields or fetching water. The Weekend Nation (published in Malawi) carried an article in 2002 on the prevalence also of rain-withholding accusations. "In a remote village in Thyolo a 65 year old man …has already been tattooed with sharp razor blades by a visiting witch-doctor, and has had to sample a bottle of liquid pepper, a measure the villagers believe would cast away his magical powers[114]. His crime? He is a prime suspect accused of withholding rains in his village because he has a kiln of unbaked bricks just outside his home." While it is not implausible that the opposite effect can occur, viz. plumes of smoke at the appropriate season inducing the formation of rain clouds, and even likely that hostile villagers may prejudice dogs against their neighbours, such beliefs do need to be distinguished from the more fantastic claims: people on planet earth do not fly on sticks at night, nor can they shrink in size (as is so commonly

---

[113] R.W.Southern: *Western Society and the Church in the Middle Ages* (Harmondsworth, 1970)

[114] Another known remedy is to throw the one who is thought to have "bound the rain" into a river, so as to "taste the flavour of the water and free what he has bound in the sky". This is presumably less common, as rivers seldom flow throughout the dry season.

believed)[115] nor make themselves invisible; it also seems unlikely that either toads or beetles are susceptible to much training; the notion of injuring or killing others, or rendering them infertile, barren or unsuccessful, by ill will alone is a singularly inconsistent theory of causation (if such is the power of the human mind, why is it otherwise so incapable?). Yet even some educated and otherwise intelligent Christian students in Zomba seem to entertain these as feasible propositions (as to some extent might those in the west who are fascinated by "unidentified flying objects", which then disappear, or whose lives are governed by their daily horoscopes).

The pity is, that such irrationality enables jealousy to find expression, thus serving again to poison community life. Even when targets of suspicion and animosity have been victimised successfully, the cycle of revenge can only continue, sometimes to the absurd extent that death is taken to be homicide except in the case of old age (when instead the deceased themselves may be reckoned to have used illicit powers!). It must be observed too, that those with any form of mental handicap or illness are the least likely to receive sympathy or understanding in a society looking for scapegoats. With HIV infection gaining so much ground, along with other disasters, there is indeed no shortage of witch-hunting. But a culture of blame, which is becoming common in western countries too, is a wholly inadequate response to many of life's misfortunes: Biblical teaching, as we have seen, suggests that it is necessary to look to one's own shortcomings, and if appropriate to accept the need for behavioural change. To this extent, the widespread occurrence of witchcraft beliefs in Africa is a major stumbling block in the prevention of HIV / AIDS.

Ancestral spirits: In 1979 the Congregation for the Doctrine of the Faith warned that "when dealing with the human situation after death, one must especially beware of arbitrary imaginative representations: excess of this kind is a major cause of difficulties that Christian faith often encounters." In fact, the Biblical survey does not fully answer the question as to which spiritual entities have the capacity to relate to the world of the living. On the whole, Hebrew thought rejects the idea that the departed are still in communication with those who are alive, and roundly condemns necromancy. This is in sharp contrast with the frequently observed African recourse to "the ancestors", and the desire to consult them or propitiate them. In this context the ancestor

---

[115] An oft-repeated story concerns miniaturized oxen: when a certain bus would not start, a diviner advised that a man carrying a small package should get off – at once allowing the engine to spring to life. Spells revealed that the man was carrying a whole herd of oxen in his package, far too heavy for the bus to pull!

means not just any forebear, but one who has lived a worthy life, dying a natural death, who was blessed with offspring and was able to provide for them. Beyond death it is believed that such a person, one of "the living dead"[116], must be richer in his ability and desire to help his kith and kin: he is closer to God than those left on earth, and his supplication therefore considered to be more effective. All this is part of the African's natural respect (alas! now gone in western society) for those who are older and more senior. Thus, if a villager wishes to request something of his village chief, he may approach him indirectly through his entourage of elders. To this extent there are elements compatible with Christian teaching, in that the saints in glory assist (Rev 5.8; 20.6), but certainly do not supercede, Christ's own intercessory prayer. But several points need to be added here. First, however much ancestors are revered, they are not necessarily saints, and earthly intercession for them may still be appropriate. John Paul II in his opening homily at the 1994 African Synod suggested that veneration of ancestors may be "in some way a preparation for belief in the communion of the saints", describing African beliefs here as "traditions open to the Gospel" and "open to the truth". Secondly, in contrast to the Church's saints, whose advocacy and support may be accessed by Christians of whatever tribe or race, resort to the ancestors is likely to be far more localized. Their partiality towards kith and kin seems to be assumed, whereas saints must surely share the universal regard of Christ himself. Thirdly, the ancestors cannot supplant the role of Christ. Criticism[117] has been levelled on this count at certain inculturated texts of the Catholic Church: the Shona burial rite, for example, in use in Zimbabwe since 1966 ascribes to the ancestors, rather than to Christ (Jn 10.9), the reception of the deceased into God's kingdom. Fourthly, it is clear that Christians have been given the *Our Father* by Jesus, a simple and direct prayer; because we are God's children we can approach him ourselves. When in our frailty words fail us, we rely upon the Holy Spirit working within us (Rom 8.26-27), who utters on our behalf Jesus' own words "Abba! Father!" (Gal 4.6); we know too that, for those who draw near to God, Christ "always lives to make intercession" (Heb 7.25). As regards claims to have

---

[116] A. Musapole in *Jesus and the Ancestors (The Lamp 18 - Balaka, Malawi, 1999)* writes: "Africans believe and therefore know that the human spirit continues to exist beyond the grave". His "therefore" is precisely the point at issue, and even if conceded allows no further deductions as to the character of such existence. The "evidence" about this is presumably thought to be conveyed in dreams, yet the Bible is insistent that the accurate interpretation of dreams is a rare gift.
[117] P.H. Gundani in *Theology Cooked in an African Pot (Zomba, 1998)*

received messages from those no longer living, the Bible suggest that what needs to be done above all is to scrutinise the content received (Deut 13.1; 1 Cor 12.1-3; 1 Jn 4.1-3) and its intended consequences (Mt 7.15-23; Lk 6.43-44). If these are consonant with God's will and purpose, then, regardless of their source, they may be regarded as reliable. What is not encouraged is following "promptings" (even if communicated in compelling dreams or visions) without critical reflection. Lastly, it must be affirmed that the singular moment of communion with the saints in heaven is actually the celebration of the Eucharist, as John the Seer so eloquently recorded in Revelation.

These examples suggest that the interaction between the Christian faith and prevailing religious or cultural beliefs means both challenge and change. The churches are challenged to discover aspects of their own heritage which have been neglected or downplayed, for example, the reality of the spiritual world, as of evil and its social and personal impact, along with family and community values. Magical beliefs and practices can remind us too of the fears and issues that haunt people's daily lives, and so deepen our pastoral resolve. Even if the symptoms of anxiety or jealousy are different in western culture from, say, the African context, the underlying malaise is often the same. Where Africans are more prone to take revenge on one another, the English response, deeply embedded even in church circles, is the refusal ever to speak or communicate again. Forgiveness comes very hard for human beings, wherever and whoever they may be. This is also the most mysterious aspect of God's own reality for anyone to understand, that at heart he is one who loves and forgives. Encounter with other religious traditions can thus re-awaken in the Christian a conviction about what is of fundamental importance in his own - although unfortunately the message preached by some churches may fail to do this, merely replacing one form of fear by another, with (for example) frequent threats of punishment and hell-fire.

It does however also imply, *mutatis mutandis*, a challenge to those other faiths or practices, beyond even what has been attempted above by way of rational critique. Fr. Chakanza in fact concludes his aforementioned article (*q.v.*) with the observation that as a result of exposure to a changing world, which includes Christian missions, indigenous ways have also altered somewhat. "It would be incorrect to think that traditional religions have survived in their original form without change. Failure to be contextually relevant leads to redundancy for any religious tradition." Even forty years earlier, in his classic study *The Primal Vision (London, 1963)*, John V. Taylor had noted how, in places where Christian influence had been at work, fear of the ancestors and their powers had become imbued with a feeling of love, along with a salvific sense of hope for them. Hence he was able to observe, "When the gaze of the living and the dead is focused on Christ himself they have less compulsive need for one another". And here one may add, that the same focus enables a more charitable, and indeed optimistic, view of one's living companions and neighbours to be taken. It has been said, "The witchcraft theory ultimately shows no faith in the convertibility of man". So Christians certainly need to challenge the stubborn belief that witches are born, not made, and to insist that, even where evil intent has been demonstrated, there can yet be remorse and a change of life. This is an issue of continuing theological concern, that popular views of God, perhaps across the world, still associate him more with creative power and retributive justice than with unconditional love and transforming grace. For too many he remains remote and detached, rather than mysteriously accessible. Likewise he is thought to impose his will through inflexible commandments, and possibly arbitrary taboos, which people disobey at their peril. The idea of being in a relationship with him that can foster personal responsibility and growth may be yet a strange idea.

The Limits of Inculturation

"Cross-cultural" communication is a very necessary part of a missionary's training. It is certainly important to realise that what is said and what is heard may sometimes be aeons apart[118]. In Lesotho in the 1980s I once noticed a student taking away from church an excessive number of palm crosses; these, he explained, were for protecting the thatch on his homestead's rondavels against God's lightning strikes from heaven[119]. That the cross symbolised at once the vulnerability of Christ and the Christ-likeness of God seemed to have escaped his attention; his own contextualisation rather exceeded its scriptural bounds. In Zomba there are perhaps some who come at the beginning of Lent to receive crosses of black ash upon their foreheads, and those too who attend Christian rites at other times, because they see it as gaining protection against harm that others may direct against them. Any moral or spiritual challenge to themselves is conveniently overlooked. I suspect that baptism of infants is

---

[118] This is familiar too within media studies, in assessing, for example, the impact of television on the developing world.

[119] Hence the Catholic *Directory on Popular Piety and the Liturgy (2002)* cautions: "Palms ... should not be kept ... for therapeutic or magical reasons to dispel evil spirits or to prevent the damage these cause in the fields or in the home."

sometimes sought for similar (protective) purposes; this is not a factor wholly absent from the rite, but distorted understanding is all too easily possible. Although the church requires all charms to be removed before the christening can proceed, these are often restored soon afterwards[120] - even though all magic and witchcraft beliefs are also explicitly renounced. Thus, while clothing the Christian liturgy in forms that correspond better with local practice is, as Paul VI famously urged[121] in 1969 in Uganda, a desirable end; it needs to be appreciated that the inner meaning of such forms can too readily be taken for granted. It follows that "the holy mysteries" of the Christian faith may sometimes be perceived as yet another kind of magic. The English equivalent, one might add, is to regard baptism as inoculation and church attendance as an insurance policy.

This is one of the toughest missionary issues, which the popularity-seeking "prosperity gospellers", promising worldly wealth, health, fame and fortune to their followers, avoid altogether. This is no new or recent phenomenon; Paul encountered it himself in Corinth, where missionary "pedlars" were reported to him as "tampering with God's word" (2 Cor 4.2), making it more congenial to their feckless hearers by omitting the demands of discipleship. No amount of inculturation can escape the truth that "the gate is narrow and the way is hard, that leads to life, and those that find it are few" (Mt 7.14). It has been said that the African, for example, will never be satisfied with a religion that does not promise him tangible rewards here and now. But that is a universal phenomenon. Here are words of a Samoan chief, noted by John Williams in 1832:-

> Only look at the English people. They have noble ships while we have only canoes. They have strong, beautiful clothes of various colours while we have only *ti* leaves; they have iron axes while we use stones; they have scissors, while we use the shark's teeth; what beautiful beads they have, looking glasses, and all that is valuable. I therefore think that the god who gave them all things must be good, and that his religion must be superior to ours. If we receive this god and worship him, he will in time give us these things as well as

---

[120] F. Kabasele Lumbala in *Celebrating Jesus Christ in Africa* describes a Congolese Catholic rite of blessing bewitched infants. He writes, "It is hard to overstate the importance of such blessings for the education of the Christian people, for bringing to them a tangible sense of the protection of God against the powers of evil, and for actually accomplishing the vanquishing of these powers".

[121] "You may, and you must, have an African Christianity."

them.[122]

Exactly these aspirations were in Samuel Pepys's mind as he sat listening nearly two hundred years earlier in the city of London:-

> A good sermon of Mr. Gifford's at our church, upon 'Seek ye first the kingdom of heaven'. A very excellent and persuasive, good and moral sermon. He showed, like a wise man, that righteousness is a surer moral way of being rich than sin and villainy.

R.L. Stevenson, writing at the start of the 20th century, commented on this passage, noting that respectable people (*sic*) like to hear "in mild accents, how you can make the most of both worlds, and be a moral hero without courage, kindness or troublesome reflection; and thus the Gospel, cleared of eastern metaphor (*i.e. inculturated for the British middle classes*), becomes a manual of worldly prudence, and a handy-book for Pepys and the successful merchant"[123]. In fact, compared with the trenchant criticisms of Soren Kierkegaard a few decades earlier, these remarks are tame: the Danish writer considered that the Church in every age has too easily mitigated the challenge of what he termed New Testament Christianity, assimilating its message to the philosophy of the day (in his day Hegelianism) and – disregarding its own other-worldliness – giving too ready a blessing to conventional this-worldly expectations.

Are the people of any continent so very different in their aspirations today? Did it not actually take Jesus two or three full years with his own disciples to persuade them otherwise, thinking as they did in all too human ways (Mk 8.31-33; 10.35ff)? Did they not still think at the end that he had failed them (Lk 24.19-21)? It is pertinent to observe that Peter's confession of faith, "You are the Christ", couched in the language of Jewish expectation, was thoroughly contextualised, but of itself remained inadequate to impart the depth of Jesus' meaning. This suggests that to portray him alternatively as *sing'anga*, ancestor or chief (within African culture), or as any kind of post-modern[124] icon or guru, may be a useful inroad into a different form of speech, but will prove to have similar limitations.

Christ is *sui generis,* and offers nothing more nor less than the gift of

---

[122] R.P. Gilson: *Samoa, 1830 to 1900 (Melbourne, 1970)*
[123] Robert Louis Stevenson: *Familiar Studies of Men and Books (New York, 1904)*
[124] The New Age temptation may be to abandon God and the person of Christ altogether, and to treat the Bible as a quarry for existentialist themes, such as 'the journey of life', 'lost innocence', 'the experience of exile', 'beauty out of ashes'. These may of course help the Gospel to establish an initial hold on minds prejudiced against it.

himself: herein lies God's mystery. Paul recognised that there is no way of preaching or commending our Lord which can ever be wholly reducible to plausible human terms: "For Jews demand signs and Greeks seek wisdom, but we preach Christ crucified, a stumbling block to Jews and folly to Gentiles" (1 Cor 1.22-23). Today some seek prosperity, while others demand protection, but what Christ offers is "not as the world gives" (Jn 14.27). It is a complete renewal of human beings and the world we inhabit: "if we have been united with him in a death like his, we shall certainly be united with him in a resurrection like his" (Rom 6.5). It is not a magical transformation achieved by cunning arts or arcane practices; it is the costly work of a God who gives himself for the life of others, and calls us to follow his example.

Bibliography

Abbot, W.M. (ed), *The Documents of Vatican II*, London: Geoffrey Chapman, 1965

Arndt, W.F. and Gingrich, F.W., *A Greek-English Lexicon*, London: University of Chicago Press, 1957

Barton, J. and Muddiman, J. (eds), *The Oxford Bible Commentary*, London: OUP. 2001

Congregation for Divine Worship, *Directory on Popular Piety and the Liturgy*, London: Catholic Truth Society, 2002

Douglas, M., *Leviticus as Literature*, Oxford: OUP, 1999

Fiedler, K., Gundani, P., and Mijoga, H. (eds), *Theology Cooked in an African Pot*, Zomba: ATISCA, 1998

Grant, R., *Gods and the one God*, London: SPCK, 1986

Hastings, A. (ed), *A World History of Christianity*, London: Cassell, 1999

Healey, J. and Sybertz, D., *Towards an African Narrative Theology*, Nairobi: Paulines Publications, 1996

Kabasele Lumbala, F., *Celebrating Jesus Christ in Africa*, New York: Orbis, 1998

Klauck, H-J., *Magic and Paganism in Early Christianity*, Edinburgh: T and T Clark, 2000

Kung, H., *Credo*, London: SCM, 1993

Lane Fox, R., *Pagans and Christians*, London: Penguin, 1988

MacQuarrie, J., *Principles of Christian Theology*, London: SCM, 1966

Maloney, R., *The Eucharist*, London: Geoffrey Chapman, 1995

Markus, R.A., *Signs and Meanings*, Liverpool: Liverpool UP, 1996

Matthews, T.F., *The Clash of Gods*, Princeton: Princeton UP, 2003

Metzger, B.M. and Coogan, M.D. (eds), *The Oxford Companion to the Bible*, New York: OUP, 1993

Nervi, L., *Malawi - Flames in the African Sky*, Balaka: Velar, 1999

Niehaus, I., *Witchcraft, Power and Politics*, London: Pluto, 2001

Petitpierre, R., *Exorcism*, London: SPCK, 1972

Shorter, A., *African Culture*, Nairobi: Paulines Publications, 1998

Soko, B., *Nchimi Chikanga, The Battle against Witchcraft in Malawi*, Blantyre: CLAIM-Kachere, 2002

Taylor, J.V., *The Primal Vision*, London: SCM, 1963

Thomas, K., *Religion and the Decline of Magic*, London: Weidenfeld and Nicolson, 1971

Van Breugel, J.W.M., *Chewa Traditional Religion*, Blantyre: CLAIM-Kachere, 2001

www.ingramcontent.com/pod-product-compliance
Lightning Source LLC
Chambersburg PA
CBHW021833300426
44114CB00009BA/427